Our Spiritual Food for Today
90 Days of Planting Seeds

Bettye A. Rowe

Copyright © 2013 Bettye A. Rowe

All rights reserved.

ISBN-10: 0989462005
ISBN-13: 978-0989462006 (Bettye Rowe)

DEDICATION

This book is dedicated to all my sisters and brothers in Christ who are in a place of uncertainty, who need some encouragement, and those that have a desire to know The Christ we serve.

I want to also dedicate this to my family, and many of my friends on Facebook, who gave me the encouragement to proceed with writing this book. I don't want to name them, but they know who they are.

My Pastor, Dayvid L. Griggs Jr. at Zion Baptist Church in Rowlett, Texas. Whom has played a huge role in my spiritual growth, and my walk with The Christ. I don't believe there would be a book titled and published, "Our Spiritual Food for Today", if I had not sat and listened to many sermons, and went to many Thursday night Bible Study sessions, under your leadership and guidance.

God truly is, The Author and Finisher of our faith!

And as strange as this may sound. I truly thank the man that broke my heart, had it not been for him breaking my heart in a way, I never thought I would recover, I would never have started writing words of encouragement and inspiration on Facebook. God definitely will turn those dark moments in our lives, and use them to make light and fire inside of us.

To my children, Stephen, Shauna, Shemesha, and Selena, your mom has finally found her passion, besides you all. Truly Blessed to be your mom, and I love you all so very much!

To my beloved mother, daddy, and brother, whom have gone home to be with The Lord. May they Rest In Love forever!

Last but not least, I thank my Heavenly Father for allowing me to be a vessel for His purpose, and not my own. I am certain, that without Him revealing Himself to me, there is no way I would be able to write anything about the Gospel of our Lord & Savior. And for that my Father, I am so grateful, and I give You all the glory, honor, and praise!

FOREWORD

The Holy Spirit put it in my heart to write a series of "Our Spiritual Food for Today" books. As I was getting ready to post on Facebook one morning, He spoke to my heart, and said, "There are many more people who can use some encouragement."

It took me a while to work up the nerve to even start to get moving with this project. But, it has been a fulfilling one! And if it will help just one person, God is pleased, and so am I.

I am just an ordinary person, that was once lost into the world. With that said, I am not a Theologian, nor a Mega Speaker, Preacher, and etc. I am just me, Bettye Rowe, who's heart God pricked, to let me know Who I belong to. I am now certain, that I belong to Him!

There will be no fancy wording, nor at times, the proper use of our English language. So, please do not use this book to teach an English class, nor Seminary; as you will be highly disappointed. It is my reflection of the Scriptures, and I have created a second page, for you to write your reflection.

Scripture says in **2 Timothy 2:15 ESV:** Do your best to present yourself to God as one approved, a worker who has no need to be ashamed, rightly handling the word of truth.

This book is to encourage, and it is in by no means a substitute for your personal Bible Study time, with The One True and Living Word of God. Hopefully, "Our Spiritual Food for Today", will encourage you to study your Bible.

And I highly recommend a Study Bible, as it will help you in so many ways with understanding the Scriptures, the timeframe of the events, and a wealth of other information, that I continue to find to be very beneficial to my spiritual growth.

ACKNOWLEDGMENTS

The Power of The Holy Trinity

The Bible

Day 1 – God Fulfills Our Needs

Good Morning my Beautiful Sunshines!

Seed: Our Spiritual Food for Today, comes from: *Philippians 4:19 ESV: And my God will supply every need of yours according to his riches in glory in Christ Jesus.*

Fruit: We like to think about God fulfilling our monetary needs; but sometimes our mental needs require God's attention.

And since we belong to Him, and He truly loves us. There are times when we really need His presence right away. There are not too many times, where I have experienced God showing up so fast, but there is one time where He showed up immediately!

Have you ever gone to church and there was this spirit that was on you, and you didn't feel like church. Don't get me wrong, I LOVE THE LORD!!! There was something on me one morning, and as I sat in the Pew during devotional, the choir was singing their first song, and I was in to it, but not really. So I started to pray, Lord get this bad spirit off of me! And please put in their hearts to sing, "How Precious Is The Name of Jesus". God answered that prayer just like that! That spirit left me in an instant.

Prior to going to church, I almost text one of the Momma Jessie that morning before church service, to ask her to sing my song! I didn't have to text her anything!

God is always right here with us, to comfort us. To give us rest when we are heavily burdened. He knows exactly what we need, and when to provide it to us. I'm not sure if I would have been any good to anybody that day, had she not sang my favorite song.

I had to let God see my inner parts, so that He could do something fast, in order to help me get back up, and continue to run this race.

When our Pianist started playing the piano, I knew immediately, that was "my song" that I love to hear her sing! And I knew that God had answered my prayer.

I know many of you may have bigger issues, but this is an example of how God operates, when we tell Him all about our troubles. He is just and faithful, to answer the prayers of those who ask Him with a sincere heart.

Be Blessed!!!

YOUR FRUIT

_____

_____

_____

_____

_____

_____

_____

_____

_____

_____

_____

_____

_____

_____

_____

_____

_____

Day 2 – A Reflection of Him

Good Morning my Beautiful Sunshines!

Seed: Our Spiritual Food for Today comes from *Galatians 3:26-28 ESV: for in Christ Jesus you are all sons of God, through faith. For as many of you as were baptized into Christ have put on Christ. There is neither Jew nor Greek, there is neither slave nor free, there is no male and female, for you are all one in Christ Jesus.*

Fruit: Once we have been baptized, and have accepted our Lord and Savior, we are now committing ourselves to strive to be exactly like Him! Meaning we can do some amazing things, just as He did! But we have to believe it, and live in the spirit, and not live in the flesh! When we live in the spirit, we don't see anything but a fellow child of God. We are blind to race, gender, social, and economic status.

The Christ doesn't put us in a category, and neither should we put each other in a category. We should be "Christ Like", instead of categorized as a particular race, and gender.

We become like minded, being on the same accord, working together to edify and glorify our Father. We humble ourselves, and seek His guidance, and direction.

Have you ever had someone in your spirit, and you picked up the phone and called them? And they tell you they are glad you called them, because they needed to hear your voice, and your voice made their day.

Our flesh cannot discern, but our spirits can!

Be Blessed!!!

YOUR FRUIT

Day 3 – A New Creature

Good Morning my Beautiful Sunshines!

Seed: Our Spiritual Food for Today, comes from: *2 Corinthians 5:17-18 ESV: Therefore, if anyone is in Christ, he is a new creation. The old has passed away; behold, the new has come. All this is from God, who through Christ reconciled us to himself and gave us the ministry of reconciliation;*

Fruit: A new creature is what we become if we are in Christ. We put away the old things we use to do, and how we use to handle old things. Some of us know the way we use to handle things were not Christ like.

Previously, if we had an ought with anyone, we wouldn't talk to them. And we would look the other way, if we saw them coming. Cuss them out, if we came in contact with them. We felt as though they wronged us somehow. We would talk about them to other people, just so folks could side with us.

As we transform into this new creation, we learn to handle things differently. We have to become the better person, and go to whoever it is, that have an ought with us, or we with them. Just as Christ reconciled us to our Father! Jesus, pleads our case to our Father, interceding daily for us. We must do the same, and reconcile them back to the same state we found them in.

If we have truly been changed for the better, our pride is set aside, we humble ourselves, love those that persecute us, and forgive one another. And we do as Christ did, when He walked the earth.

It is the only way to please our Father, it sets us free when we reconcile our differences, and any ought we have against someone.

Be Blessed!!!

YOUR FRUIT

Day 4 – Love Covers A Multitude of Sin

Good Morning my Beautiful Sunshines!

Seed: Our Spiritual Food for Today, comes from *1 John 4:20-21 ESV: If anyone says, "I love God," and hates his brother, he is a liar; for he who does not love his brother whom he has seen cannot love God whom he has not seen. And this commandment we have from him: whoever loves God must also love his brother.*

Fruit: We cannot love God, and not love our fellow brothers, sisters, neighbors, strangers, coworkers, and enemies! It is a commandment that we love everybody! It is one of the Ten Commandments in the old testament, and also when Jesus gave a new Commandment to His Disciples, in John 13:34 ESV: *A new commandment I give unto you, That ye love one another; as I have loved you, that ye also love one another.*

We can't harbor bitterness and hatred for our fellow brothers and sisters. These types of characteristics clearly let us know that such, is not a part of God. These are evil characteristics, and they will have us bound in chains. If Jesus withstood all that He endured, surely we can love each other. And yes, we get talked about, mistreated, but it is nothing compared to what Jesus went thru. And He still asked our Father to forgive those that crucified Him.

Just so you know; love is an action word, and not a word that can only be talked about. When we love one another, God moves in our lives. He takes notice to the love we have for one another, and for Him.

Be Blessed!!!

YOUR FRUIT

Day 5 – Die Daily

Good Morning my Beautiful Sunshines!

Seed: Our Spiritual Food for Today, comes from: ***Galatians 5:16 ESV: But I say, walk by the Spirit, and you will not gratify the desires of the flesh.***

Fruit: It is so easy for our flesh to take over and consume our thoughts, the way we feel, and the way we talk. When we live in the spirit, we realize that what we see and feel with the physical eye, and body; it is only a distraction. But thanks to our Lord & Savior, He left with us The Comforter, The Holy Spirit! He helps us to walk upright, and He convicts us when we allow our flesh to get distracted.

The Holy Spirit is incapable of sinning! It's the flesh that makes us weak, and our flesh is the leading cause of our sins! The Apostle Paul says in **1 Corinthians 15:31**, we have to die daily to the flesh! I know it is a constant battle, but we have to put on the whole armor of Christ to run this race! The enemy is seeking to steal, kill, and destroy all of our promises! And if we allow ourselves to walk in the flesh, and not die to it; the enemy will have accomplished, what he set out to do.

Don't give the enemy that satisfaction! We belong to God, and we need to really keep our eyes on life eternal! These bodies will return to dust, but that new resurrected body will live forever.

Just remember, temporary pleasure, can, and will bring eternal pain!

Be Blessed!!!

YOUR FRUIT

Day 6 – What Are You Sowing

Good Morning my Beautiful Sunshines!

Seed: Our Spiritual Food for Today, comes from: *Galatians 6:7-8 ESV: Do not be deceived: God is not mocked, for whatever one sows, that will he also reap. For the one who sows to his own flesh will from the flesh reap corruption, but the one who sows to the Spirit will from the Spirit reap eternal life.*

Fruit: We can fool some people when we put on that mask. How many of you know that we will never be able to deceive our Father? No matter how we try and disguise our tricks, deceit, jealousy, and envy. We will never be able to hide anything from God.

Why should we care more about our flesh, than our spirit? It is our spirit's that God speaks to. If we live in the spirit, we don't lose sight of where we are going. If we care more about our flesh, our focus will be more on worldly things, and these things will consume and corrupt us. Therefore, we will do anything to anybody to feed our flesh, and to gain what our flesh desires.

If we choose to feed our flesh more than our spirit; our flesh will dominate our will to surrender and submit to our Father.

We need to constantly feed our spirit man with The Word, prayer, meditation of The Word, and developing the Fruits of The Spirit. We need to feed our spirit with positive food. The Word is our bread when we are hungry, and our drink when we are thirsty. It's spiritual food, and we will never have to go hungry or thirst again. As long as we continually feed our spirits The Word of God.

And it is written. When we sow to the Spirit, we will reap life everlasting!

Be Blessed!!!

YOUR FRUIT

Day 7 – It Shall Be Done

Good Morning my Beautiful Sunshines!

Seed: Our Spiritual Food for Today, comes from *Matthew 7:7-8 ESV: "Ask, and it will be given to you; seek, and you will find; knock, and it will be opened to you. For everyone who asks receives, and the one who seeks finds, and to the one who knocks it will be opened.*

Fruit: Just ask, seek, and knock! It SHALL be given to you! You SHALL find it! It SHALL be opened! Jesus didn't say it could, or maybe, or a possibility! HE said SHALL! Just remember, it may not be immediately, but when we are ready for it! HE is just waiting on us to come to Him with a humble heart, and a bowed head!

After you have asked, exercise your faith and have no doubt that God will give to you, you will find it, and He will open it for you.

Our prayers are never returned void.

However, we need to make sure whatever we ask for, we are ready to receive. We may think we are ready, but our Father, doesn't. And when He feels that we are not ready, He will delay our "yes", until He continues to work in us, and prepare us to be ready to receive what it is we prayed to Him about.

And please make sure we are not praying for the wrong thing, or person. Because once we receive what it is we asked God for, He will give it to us. And we may find out, it was not all what it was cracked up to be. So we must keep what it is we asked for.

But once we pray for a spiritual Blessing, or something, or someone that will help us, or enhance us, these are the things He prepares us for. And the things, and/or person we are grateful and thankful for.

Be Blessed!!!

YOUR FRUIT

Day 8 – Pray In Secret

Good Morning my Beautiful Sunshines!

Seed: Our Spiritual Food for Today, comes from: *Matthew 6:6 ESV: But when you pray, go into your room and shut the door and pray to your Father who is in secret. And your Father who sees in secret will reward you.*

Fruit: Our personal prayers to our Father should only be between us, and our Father in Heaven. I've been guilty of this myself. And I've seen others who are on social media write a prayer for healing, deliverance, and etc. But once I read this scripture, and was reminded of it, by The Holy Spirit, I no longer write or say a prayer in public.

God wants you to tell Him all about your troubles, your joys, and what it is you are asking Him for, or would like Him to do, in private. He doesn't want us to share everything with others. Some things are between our Father, and you.

What He wants to give you, is only for you! So we need to be careful about making a public request, which should only be between you, and our Father.

Also, some of us have overflow, which is God's favor! Pray for your fellow man whom may be going thru, and can use a Blessing!

Transfer some of that favor to them! God allows it!

Be Blessed!!!

YOUR FRUIT

Day 9 – One God, The Truth

Good Morning my Beautiful Sunshines!

Seed: Our Spiritual Food for Today, comes from: *Deuteronomy 6:4-5 ESV: "Hear, O Israel: The LORD our God, the LORD is one. You shall love the LORD your God with all your heart and with all your soul and with all your might.*

Fruit: We can only serve and love God, not another god, and it is my hope that it is The True and Living God that you serve. Trying to straddle the fence, clearly means we don't love God with all our heart, soul, and might. There is a great reward for those that love and serve our Father with our all.

There is peace, comfort, protection, love, and a home in Heaven; when we love God, and acknowledge Him as our only True God.

There is nothing, or no one that can compare to our Father! The Israelites had to learn the hard way. They had lack of patience, complained, they didn't want to obey God, unless He did something for them. And I'm sure we can attest to the mindset of the Israelites. I know I have been guilty of this, myself. Only praising God when he does something for me.

One should not discount God, as being our temporary fix, when He is our permanent solution to every trouble, trial, and situation we are faced with.

He just want us to serve Him, and Him only! Once the Israelites surrendered to His will and way, He delivered them from bondage. Please know that He will do the same for us.

We should love Him with our whole heart. Actually this is a commandment, so we are required to. See also, **Matthew 22:37**.

Be Blessed!!!

YOUR FRUIT

Day 10 – Paradise In Heaven

Good Morning my Beautiful Sunshines!

Seed: Our Spiritual Food for Today, comes from: *1 Corinthians 2:9 ESV: But, as it is written, "What no eye has seen, nor ear heard, nor the heart of man imagined, what God has prepared for those who love him"—*

Fruit: Our thoughts and minds can't even imagine what God has prepared for us on the other side, for those who love Him! The most beautiful things we see here on this side, cannot compare to His Kingdom in Heaven!

We have seen many beautiful mansions, cars, and vacation spots; but even these beautiful and wonderful things; and as breath taking some of these places are, they can't compare to what God has prepared for His children that love and obey Him.

So ask yourself! Why should I worry about not having nice things on this side? So what, if I don't live in a mansion, or drive a nice car, and can't go to a breath taking vacation spot, where the water is just amazing!

There are folks who will sell their souls, and do anything to live in a mansion, drive nice cars, wear the finest clothes, and jewelry. But, these are things that will corrupt, and will pass away.

Just know, if we endure to the very end, that our home on the other side is something so amazing, that our mind can't even grasp the beauty of it.

Be Blessed!!!

YOUR FRUIT

Day 11 – Our Works

Good Morning my Beautiful Sunshines!

Seed: Our Spiritual Food for Today, comes from: *1 Thessalonians 1:1-3 ESV: Paul, Silvanus, and Timothy, To the church of the Thessalonians in God the Father and the Lord Jesus Christ: Grace to you and peace. We give thanks to God always for all of you, constantly mentioning you in our prayers, remembering before our God and Father your work of faith and labor of love and steadfastness of hope in our Lord Jesus Christ.*

Fruit: I like the way Paul addresses the Church of Thessalonians. He begins with Thanksgiving of our Father, and how the Thessalonians faith, love, and work shows he is pleased!

They were hungry and receptive to pleasing, and following our Lord! Just as we do, when God get our attention. We are compelled to do all that is pleasing in His sight!

Our good works, and faith will be recorded in the Lamb's Book of Life. Everything that we do, is recorded; both good and bad. We should want to be acknowledged and rewarded for the good deeds, our love for Christ, our obedience, and works to be the determining factor of where our permanent home will be, after we leave this side.

Just remember, only what we do for The Christ will last, and will matter. We should do all things in love, and without grumbling, and complaining.

Be Blessed!!!

YOUR FRUIT

Day 12 – Perfect Love Has No Fear

Good Morning my Beautiful Sunshines!

Seed: Our Spiritual Food for Today, comes from: *1 John 4:18 ESV: There is no fear in love, but perfect love casts out fear. For fear has to do with punishment, and whoever fears has not been perfected in love.*

Fruit: We all say we want to experience real love, but often times it seems that when someone shows us love by their actions, we tend to sabotage that love. Many of us have this fear that we will eventually get hurt, by the ones that show us love. It is constantly in the back of our minds that something is not right, and no one could love us this much, so there must be a motive. Thus we act out on that fear, by showing the ugliness we have inside of us.

We allow the enemy to deceive us; he whispers in our ear that the ones that love us, are not that loving person they are portraying. And when we act on what the enemy whispered to us, we show the ugly side, and we are expecting the ones that love us to do the same. Sometimes they will react to the negativity we dish out, and this gives us a reason to call it quits. This is the torment of this fear of love. Never fully capable of trusting, or receiving love.

But that love of Jesus for us, His perfect love; there was no fear when He stayed on The Cross! Fulfilling the greatest act of love known to all mankind! No questions, no regrets.

Can you imagine how life would be, if we loved each other, with the same perfect love that Jesus have for us?

One day, we will!

Be Blessed!!!

YOUR FRUIT

Day 13 – Fear Is Not In Our Genetic Make Up

Good Morning my Beautiful Sunshines!

Seed: Our Spiritual Food for Today, comes from: *2 Timothy 1:7 ESV: for God gave us a spirit not of fear but of power and love and self-control.*

Fruit: God has gifted unto each of us, spiritual gifts. Some have the gift of laying of hands to heal, singing, playing a musical instrument, teaching, and so many other gifts. Some of us share the same spiritual gifts, and some of us are equipped with more than one spiritual gift.

Do not be afraid to use your spiritual gift, as you never know who it will help. But when you use it, and others see your wonderful gift, do not get prideful and arrogant. Have the self-control to know when to use it, and when not to. Always allow The Holy Spirit to be your guide.

God gave us a gift for His glory, and purpose, and not of that of our own. We need to stir up the gifts that God has placed inside of us, and not allow it to sit idle. What good would we be to anyone if we didn't use our gift?

When I hear The Word being preached really well, without The Word being watered down, taken out of context, it does my soul and spirit something wonderful! It's because that person that preach The Word is pouring out of them, what God has poured into them. It is genuine, and they allow The Holy Spirit to increase within them.

Remember self-control, love, and humility is of God. No control, self-righteousness, self-gratification is not of God.

What are we using our spiritual gifts for? Self or for the edification of our Father in Heaven?

Be Blessed!!!

YOUR FRUIT

Day 14 – The Power Of Words

Good Morning my Beautiful Sunshines!

Seed: Our Spiritual Food for Today, comes from: ***Psalms 120:1 ESV: In my distress I called to the LORD, and he answered me.*** In verse 2 David continues to say. ***Deliver me, O LORD, from lying lips, from a deceitful tongue.***

Fruit: David was crying out because those that smiled in his face, talked behind his back. Whoa, how many people do we know do us the same way? It gets a bit much and we have to cry out to God to deliver us from lying tongues, deceitful people who know they don't have our best interest!

Be careful not to fall prey in doing the same thing, and partake into these tongues with busy bodies!

Our mouth and tongue can literally give life to someone, or death to someone!

Doesn't it feel good, and lift our spirits, when people are encouraging, and have nice things to say to us, and about us?

But, on the other hand. When someone only speaks negative things about us, tear us down, instead of building us up; it grieves the spirit. And it can be depressing, as we feel as though they may be correct with what they say, because that's all we hear! Their words kill us slowly!

But when we know better we do better! Meaning, when someone wants to tear us down, we should just pray for them. Keep it moving, because we don't need these type of people in our lives! We know we are not who they say we are. So they don't matter. Only what God thinks about us, is all that matters.

Be Blessed!!!

YOUR FRUIT

Day 15 – Our Answers Are Sometimes Delayed

Good Morning my Beautiful Sunshines!

Seed: Our Spiritual Food for Today, comes from: ***Daniel 10:12-13 ESV: Then he said to me, "Fear not, Daniel, for from the first day that you set your heart to understand and humbled yourself before your God, your words have been heard, and I have come because of your words. The prince of the kingdom of Persia withstood me twenty-one days, but Michael, one of the chief princes, came to help me, for I was left there with the kings of Persia,***

Fruit: In spite of all that we go thru! The test & trials, disappointments, hurt, and pain! Whatever it is? Know that God hear our cries, and we need to let Him take control! When we try to fix things, and take matters in to our own hands, we really mess things up. We do this because we feel as thou God does not care!

Take this scripture and meditate on it! God hear our cries and prayers the moment we speak them. Just know the enemy will do all he can to block those prayers.

Michael, the Archangel had to fight with the fallen angel just to bring Daniel God's response! Michael was held up for 21 days!

But that's great news, because we have God's Angels fighting a spiritual warfare for us, as God's Angels love us as well. They are faithful in their obedience to our Father!

Just remember to keep praying, and keep the faith! And know that your answer is on its way.

Be Blessed!!!

YOUR FRUIT

Day 16 – Jesus Alone

Good Morning my Beautiful Sunshines!

Seed: Our Spiritual Food for Today, comes from: *Matthew 27:45 ESV: Now from the sixth hour there was darkness over all the land until the ninth hour.*

Fruit: Something that made me have a "WOW" moment in Discipleship training one evening! GOD is ABSOLUTE in HIS RIGHTEOUSNESS!!! HE even turned away from our Lord & Savior, Jesus, when He bore the sins of the world at Calvary on that rugged cross! Just think, He didn't even show Jesus mercy, He could have, but He didn't! Why? I'm glad you asked!

God can't stand sin, it stinks to His nostrils, and because Jesus took on all our sins, He who knew no sin, became sin, and it stank to God. It didn't matter that Jesus was God's only Begotten Son, the only One who could bring Salvation to the world!

This should let us know that the inconceivable love God have for us! So much so, that He would turn away from Jesus at this most darkest hour. When I'm sure Jesus needed Him the most. God showed Jesus no mercy! But think about the mercy and grace God shows us daily! When we can't even compare to Jesus!

Please give God some of your time! He is so worthy! He doesn't deserve to be ignored. It is sad, that the only time we seek Him out, or acknowledge Him, is when we need Him!

We are so behind on our praises to our Father! We have to stop taking Him for granted!

Be Blessed!!!

YOUR FRUIT

Day 17 – Forgiveness In The Midst of Dying

Good Morning my Beautiful Sunshines!

Seed: Our Spiritual Food for Today, comes from: ***Luke 23:34 ESV:* And Jesus said, "Father, forgive them, for they know not what they do." And they cast lots to divide his garments.**

Fruit: My Pastor said something one Sunday morning during church service! Another WOW moment!!! "Jesus paused death to intercede for those who were persecuting Him. "Forgive them Father, for they know not what they do!"

Jesus was spit on, scourged, beaten, and mocked. The natural man would have wanted to return evil for evil, but Jesus was supernatural. Meaning He returned good for evil.

So family, when others persecute you, by any means; will you pause and intercede on their behalf. Ask our Father to forgive them, for they know not what they do! But not only intercede on their behalf, be Christ like, and get in the spirit of returning good for evil.

Recognize that what dwells in them needs to be removed, and it is not of God. We have to pray for our enemies; and intercede for them!

Why would we want to ask for forgiveness for someone who hurts us? This is our natural man, who would want to return evil for evil.

Often times, the ones who are hurting us mentally, or physically, are hurting as well. And since we are strong in our faith, we should know better than to battle evil with evil. Instead we pray for them. We don't have to continue to take it, and live with abuse, but we should pray for them.

Remember, this is a spiritual warfare. But, we must also realize, that good will always defeat evil!

Prayer changes things. And I've witnessed people who have been the abuser, go back to the person they abused, and asked for their forgiveness.

Now this is what the power of prayer, living in the spirit, and forgiveness can do.

Be Blessed!!!

YOUR FRUIT

Day 18 – Steps of A Good Man

Good Morning my Beautiful Sunshines!

Seed: Our Spiritual Food for Today, comes from: *Psalm 37:23-24 ESV: The steps of a man are established by the LORD, when he delights in his way; though he fall, he shall not be cast head long, for the LORD upholds his hand.*

Fruit: When our steps are ordered by God, we may at times feel like we can't go any further. We feel like giving up, and sitting on the side lines. And at times we may fall, but we won't stay down.

Have you ever felt like all hope is gone when you have tried to do something positive for your life? And it seems like the more you try, there is always something, or someone that knocks us off our path.

But there is something bigger than us, Who will not allow us to quit. It is the hands of God, that gives us the strength to keep moving forward. Picking us back up, and guiding our every step.

You see, often times, God gives us direction, but we will try and take short cuts. Because the path that He has instructed us to follow, seems to be too long, and too hard. This is when we fall, as we want to take short cuts. But when we allow God to take control, although not an easy path, but one we learn to be happy to endure, because of all those past bruises.

As long as we keep pressing on, He will uphold us with His hands.

Stay focused on the reward!

Be Blessed!!!

YOUR FRUIT

Day 19 – Train Up A Child

Good Morning my Beautiful Sunshines!

Seed: Our Spiritual Food for Today, comes from: *Proverbs 22:6 ESV: Train up a child in the way he should go; even when he is old he will not depart from it.*

Fruit: So many times I've heard the following scripture misquoted.

Some seem to leave out "and when he is old". I use to scratch my head, and say to myself, what am I doing wrong as a parent?

When I read this scripture for myself, it hit me! Our kids are no different than we are, when we were their age. Well, most of us anyway. We were no saints, and we tried to get over on our parents also! Often times succeeding!

But even then, our parents planted that seed of introducing us to Jesus, by taking us to church, making us say grace before we eat, and saying our prayers at night.

It's true the older we get, the wiser we become. Well some of us anyway. We came back to what was planted inside of us!

To put God first in our lives, and He will take care of us! We will surely have trials, but it is so much better when we let The Word be our guide!

And if we live to see adulthood, we have our parents, and grandparents to thank. They were the angels that prayed for us, while we were out in the world, and making the mistakes our children make. Praying for our covering, and for God to put up His hedge of protection around us.

Don't be too hard on your children, when they make mistakes. But do tell them about our Lord & Savior, Jesus, The Christ.

Oh, and don't send them to church without you accompanying them. We need to be an active participant as well. Be a good example for them. Because if we don't someone else will show them the wrong way. And when they do grow up, the training they received when they were younger, is the lifestyle that will be hard for them to flee from.

Be Blessed!!!

YOUR FRUIT

Day 20 – God Heals The Broken Hearted

Good Morning my Beautiful Sunshines!

Seed: Our Spiritual Food for Today, comes from: **Psalms 34:18 ESV:** *The LORD is near to the brokenhearted and saves the crushed in spirit.*

Fruit: Time heals all wounds! How many times have we heard this saying?

When we have been injured by a cut, sprained something, or tore something on our bodies; that injury eventually heals. Day by day, the injury gets better when we care for it, or someone who loves us care for it.

Although there may be a scar there, it simply reminds us of how we got that scar. And often times we tell a story to others how we got that scar, and we laugh about it.

Our hearts are no different, when we are hurt by someone mentally, and when we let go of that hurt, with time our hearts heal! Day by day, that pain fades away! And one day, we begin to share and laugh again with others. Even laugh and talk jokingly about the one that hurt us!

The key to healing, just as a wound on our body, is to care for it, do what it takes to not re-injure it, because if we constantly pick at the injury the longer it takes to heal.

Learn to trust God with that broken heart. He draws near to us, to help us with the healing process. It is Him that tells us to not beat ourselves up, over the mistake we made.

But don't keep picking at, or messing with the same one that broke your heart! Let him or her go!

One day it will be just a memory that will no longer have you in bondage!

Be Blessed!!!

YOUR FRUIT

Day 21 – God Chasten Those He Love

Good Morning my Beautiful Sunshines!

Seed: Our Spiritual Food for Today, comes from: *Hebrews 12:6 ESV: For the Lord disciplines the one he loves, and chastises every son whom he receives."*

I will also include **Hebrews** 12:*7-8 ESV: It is for discipline that you have to endure. God is treating you as sons. For what son is there whom his father does not discipline? If you are left without discipline, in which all have participated, then you are illegitimate children and not sons.*

Fruit: No matter how old my children are, if I see something that grieves my spirit, I have to call them on it! Imagine what it does to God! I will correct the ones I gave birth to, because I love them, just as God loves us!

If we are His, He chastise us, and as much as it is necessary! God can't have His children doing all kinds of ungodly things, and think we will receive favor with Him! That's not how He operates. I'm not God, but I do care and love my children, as well as their souls!

If I didn't love and care for my children, I wouldn't say a word when they are doing things they shouldn't be doing, and speaking in a disrespectful manner. It's called respect; to themselves, and to others.

God will not hold back the chastening on us, because He loves us! And we will definitely walk upright when God get a hold of us. We grow tired of His chastening, and have no choice but to want to be in His good grace.

No matter how old mine get, I will tell them what thus sayeth The Lord! He certainly don't put an age limit on us, as we are His children forever.

Be Blessed!!!

YOUR FRUIT

Day 22 – For His Purpose

Good Morning my Beautiful Sunshines!

Seed: Our Spiritual Food for Today, comes from: *Romans 8:28 ESV: And we know that for those who love God all things work together for good, for those who are called according to his purpose.*

Fruit: Yes, ALL things work together, the good and the bad. There is a reason we have trials and tribulations. He is preparing us for our purpose, for Him.

For those of us who love God, we have the faith that God will see us though. God test our very hearts to see how we react to certain situations, and if we truly love Him as we proclaim, we will carry our cross soberly, patiently, and steadily.

If we never went through anything, would we really give God His praises? Would we ever acknowledge Him?

We should rejoice that God loves us so much, that He allows us to experience both good and bad things.

This should let us know that we belong to Him, and He has called us to assist Him with building His Kingdom.

Each test and trial that we bear and overcome, it builds our confidence, increases our faith, our strength, it humbles us, and it is a testimony to be shared with others.

We don't think we are the only one who experience similar trials and tribulations, do we? We may have just came out our storm, and someone we may cross paths with, will be going into theirs. And we minister to them, pray with them, show compassion to them, because we've been there.

They see the light of The Christ in us, so they know they to, can endure it.

And who gets the glory?

That's right! God!

Be Blessed!!!

YOUR FRUIT

Day 23 – Fruits To Labor

Good Morning my Beautiful Sunshines!

Seed: Our Spiritual Food for Today, comes from: *2 Peter 1:5-8 ESV: For this very reason, make every effort to supplement your faith with virtue, and virtue with knowledge, and knowledge with self-control, and self-control with steadfastness, and steadfastness with godliness, and godliness with brotherly affection, and brotherly affection with love. For if these qualities are yours and are increasing, they keep you from being ineffective or unfruitful in the knowledge of our Lord Jesus Christ.*

Fruit: Without being diligent, there is no gaining of holiness! How do we expect to be transformed, and be of service to anyone else, if we are not diligent in our studies? Not only diligent, but we have to make some sacrifices. Learn self-control, and deny our fleshly desires. Not only am I talking about a relationship with someone, but also the things we use to do. Like watching television often, or hanging out with friends and family. We have to give more of our time to reading, studying, and gaining knowledge of our Lord & Savior.

If we have committed ourselves to be a living vessel for God, we cannot slumber. We have to be prepared and ready to answer. For, *1 Peter 3:15 ESV:* says, **but in your hearts honor Christ the Lord as holy, always being prepared to make a defense to anyone who asks you for a reason for the hope that is in you; yet do it with gentleness and respect,**

We can't lead, nor transform anyone to become believers in our Lord & Savior, if we don't fully understand our reason for being a Christian (Christ like). We are to defend our belief, but we need to defend it with gentleness and respect. And this my friends, is a work in progress for me at times. Defending my belief in our Savior with gentleness, that is to say. The "respectful" I can handle, but it is very difficult for me to be gentle when someone is being negative and downright ugly about our Lord & Savior, Jesus. Self-control is definitely needed.

But when we seek after our Lord with great diligence, we will learn to be like Him. In the manner of our faith being increased, virtue, knowledge, self-control, steadfastness, godliness, brotherly affection, and love. Being a highly effective and fruitful servant for His purpose!

When these qualities are increased; the Heavens rejoice, and the enemy gets mad!

Be Blessed!!!

YOUR FRUIT

_____

_____

_____

_____

_____

_____

_____

_____

_____

_____

_____

_____

_____

_____

_____

Day 24 – Praise Him Before The Rocks Do

Good Morning my Beautiful Sunshines!

Seed: Our Spiritual Food for Today, comes from: *Luke 19:39-40 ESV: And some of the Pharisees in the crowd said to him, "Teacher, rebuke your disciples." He answered, "I tell you, if these were silent, the very stones would cry out."*

Fruit: There is a song that says, "Never Will A Rock Cry Out In My Place."

We were not there when Jesus walked the earth, ministered, healed, taught, and nurtured His people over 2000 years ago. But, just to mention, and read about all that He did, how could we not give such a wonderful, amazing, compassionate, giver, teacher, healer, and deliverer all our praises?

If you haven't experienced the goodness, and power of The Christ, I urge you to seek Him out, and experience Him for yourself.

Once you have eaten from His plate, and have drank from His cup, you will never hunger or thirst for anyone, or anything else.

If you are like me, and have experienced His love and kindness for yourself, you will know what I am talking about. He sits at the Right Hand of our Father, interceding and mediating on our behalf, daily.

He is that peace that dwells within us, that surpasses all our understanding! An indescribable joy!

Our comfort when we are lonely! Simply Amazing, He is!

How could we ever allow some rocks to take our place in giving Him praises!

Be Blessed!!!

YOUR FRUIT

Day 25 – Planted By God

Good Morning my Beautiful Sunshines!

Seed: Our Spiritual Food for Today, comes from: *Jeremiah 17:7-8 ESV: "Blessed is the man who trusts in the LORD, whose trust is the LORD. He is like a tree planted by water, that sends out its roots by the stream, and does not fear when heat comes, for its leaves remain green, and is not anxious in the year of drought, for it does not cease to bear fruit."*

Fruit: We shall not be moved nor destroyed, and there is nothing, or no one, who will be able to take our light away, because of what has been planted inside of us. Our fruits will continually flourish!

We may get picked of our fruits every once in a while, and someone may even try to cut us down. But the roots that God gave us will only produce more fruit, and grow bigger, taller, and stronger.

Nothing or no one can remove the roots of God! People can try to dig them up all they wish, but when we are planted by God, we can't be moved!

The spirit is that seed that gives us those roots that will sustain a raging thunderstorm.

Be blessed!!!

YOUR FRUIT

Day 26 – The Whole Armor

Good Morning my Beautiful Sunshines!

Seed: Our Spiritual Food for Today, comes from: ***Ephesians 6:10-11 ESV: Finally, be strong in the Lord and in the strength of his might. Put on the whole armor of God, that you may be able to stand against the schemes of the devil.***

Fruit: We can't stand against the wits, and cunningness of the enemy without the whole armor of God, half just won't do. Remember satan was an angel before he fell from grace, and he knows where his destiny is. He desires to take as many of us, with him as he can.

The enemy will tempt us with a many of things, but remember it's just things! God's children are to not be conformed to this world because it will surely perish and all its contents! When we put on the mindset of Christ Jesus the enemy will not be able to tempt us!

And believe me, the enemy knows what our weaknesses are, and he will present them to us, all nicely. Some of us will take the bait, removing ourselves from the armor of God.

But after the enemy has riddled us with bullets of deception, we seek out the armor and protection of our Father. It's best to stay there, and to keep on His armor, which is by studying His Word.

Remember, satan made 3 efforts to tempt Jesus, but even at Jesus most weakest moment, He still resisted the devil!

And we are to resist him also. But we have to be equipped with The armor of The Christ.

Be Blessed!!!

YOUR FRUIT

Day 27 – Receive The Crown of Life

Good Morning my Beautiful Sunshines!

Seed: Our Spiritual Food for Today, comes from: *James 1:12 ESV: Blessed is the man who remains steadfast under trial, for when he has stood the test he will receive the crown of life, which God has promised to those who love him.*

Fruit: As long as we are on this side, trials and tribulations will surely come our way. It is how we respond that matters when we are faced with trials. Our response will either please God, or it will not. If we do not pass the test, we can be sure it will come around again, and again. Until we have matured and know how to endure the trials we face.

Should we grow weary, and want to throw in the towel, there is a name we can call that will carry us! His Name is above all names, and that my friends, is Jesus.

But once we realize that the trials that come our way, are only to increase our faith, and trust in God. We take on a whole new mindset. No longer do we grow weary, and want to faint; but praise Him in the mist of the storm.

I can recall in Scripture, where God asked the enemy have he considered testing His good and faithful servant Job? And how wonderful God must have felt that Job would be able to withstand what was to come upon him.

This is how God feels about us as well. We are letting Him know that we trust Him, and in spite of all that we are enduring, we will continue to praise His Holy Name.

We know what we will receive if we just trust Him, and endure until the end.

There is nothing better on this earth, than to get into Heaven and have God crown us with eternal life!

Be Blessed!!!

YOUR FRUIT

Day 28 – Persecuted For His Name

Good Morning my Beautiful Sunshines!

Seed: Our Spiritual Food for Today, comes from: *Philippians 1:29 ESV: For it has been granted to you that for the sake of Christ you should not only believe in him but also suffer for his sake,*

Fruit: Faith and salvation is free indeed. Although we were not living when our Lord and Savior Jesus, witnessed, taught, performed miracles, raise the dead, and bore the sins of the world. Yet we believe He did these things because of our Faith.

Non-believers, unbelievers, and some who say they believe will persecute us because of the expression of our faith. It's ok, because this scripture clearly states we should suffer for His name! *2 Timothy 3:12* says, **Yea, and all that will live godly in Christ Jesus shall suffer persecution. Matthew 24:9 Jesus says: Then shall they deliver you to be afflicted, and shall kill you: and yet shall be hated of all nations for my name's sake.**

It should be no surprise that those who love Jesus and spread the good news of His greatness will be persecuted, and hated.

So just as Jesus, if we endure to the end on this side, we will receive a great reward from our Father in Heaven on the other side.

Be blessed!!!

YOUR FRUIT

Day 29 – Who Covers You

Good Morning my Beautiful Sunshines!

Seed: Our Spiritual Food for Today, comes from: *Psalm 62:7 ESV: On God rests my salvation and my glory; my mighty rock, my refuge is God.*

Fruit: God can only give us salvation, man can't give us that. Not even the most popular of men/women.

There is a song that says, "God is my everything." He is our all in all: strength, that rock in a weary land, healer, provider, way maker, refuge, comforter, peace, unconditional lover, chastiser, Father, lifeline, and so much more.

Man may, or can give us temporary comfort, but God's gifts are everlasting! It would behoove us to stay with what is tried and true! And that is our Father! Glory is for Him, and comes from Him.

And only Jesus, The Christ ushered in salvation, and that my loves, is free, and just for the asking!

Never be fooled by man, who will entice you to turn from God. Let them know, there is nothing they can give you, that is, nor ever will be greater than what God can give you; us.

Be Blessed!!!

YOUR FRUIT

Day 30 – Only One

Good Morning my Beautiful Sunshines!

Seed: Our Spiritual Food for Today, comes from: *1 Timothy 2:5-6 ESV: For there is one God, and there is one mediator between God and men, the man Christ Jesus, who gave himself as a ransom for all, which is the testimony given at the proper time.*

Fruit: Meditate on the first sentence! Only ONE GOD! And that's what that is! Exodus 32 When Moses came down from the mountain the Israelites had made their own god, because of their being impatient! God plagued His children for their actions, being disobedient, by serving another "god".

Also note that there is only ONE Mediator between God and men! Only Jesus can mediate and intercede to our Father on our behalf! Sure we can intercede to Jesus for our brothers and sisters, but it is Jesus alone that can present our prayers to our Father!

John 14:6 ESV: Jesus said to him, "I am the way, and the truth, and the life. No one comes to the Father except through me.

Oh, and there is no other way to get to Heaven either!

Jesus, The Christ is the only One that was found worthy!

Be Blessed!!!

YOUR FRUIT

Day 31 – He Knew No Sin

Good Morning my Beautiful Sunshines!

Seed: Our Spiritual Food for Today, comes from: *2 Corinthians 5:21 ESV: For our sake he made him to be sin who knew no sin, so that in him we might become the righteousness of God.*

Fruit: That means God loved us so much, that He allowed His only Begotten Son to bear His wrath, for sinners like us. To descend from the Heavens, fashion a physical body, lower Himself, and become a servant to us.

This is God's inconceivable love for us! I don't know about you, but I have yet to grasp my mind around how much God loves us. Why would He allow His Son to go through all the anguish, hatred, and abuse that Jesus went through? When it is apparent, that many of us take God's love for granted, and when many don't believe.

But yet, and still, He desires to have a wonderful and meaningful relationship with each one of us.

Now that's true and unconditional love!

Allowing sweet Jesus to become sin, when He knew no sin! Sin was nowhere in Him!

Father, I say THANK YOU!

Be Blessed!!!

YOUR FRUIT

Day 32 – Rejected By Man

Good Morning my Beautiful Sunshines!

Seed: Our Spiritual Food for Today, comes from: *Isaiah 53:3-4 ESV: He was despised and rejected by men; a man of sorrows, and acquainted with grief; and as one from whom men hide their faces he was despised, and we esteemed him not. Surely he has borne our griefs and carried our sorrows; yet we esteemed him stricken, smitten by God, and afflicted.*

Fruit: The One that was rejected by men, bore their/our grief, sorrow, frustrations, and all other afflictions; He carried them all! Yet, we do not give Jesus our all, considering everything He did and continue to do for us!

They thought surely, this is not the Son of God, He is a mere carpenter, and look at His family. He can't be! Man, were they wrong!!!

Jesus is our daily Mediator, reminding our Father of what He did in exchange for our short comings! He constantly intercedes on our behalf, when we go to Him and ask for forgiveness of our sins. And whatever it is, that we petition our Father for.

Tell someone about Jesus, don't be ashamed of who He is, what He's done for us, and what He can do!

Be Blessed!!!

YOUR FRUIT

Day 33 – The Author of Our Faith

Good Morning my Beautiful Sunshines!

Seed: Our Spiritual Food for Today comes from: *Hebrews 12:2 ESV: looking to Jesus, the founder and perfecter of our faith, who for the joy that was set before him endured the cross, despising the shame, and is seated at the right hand of the throne of God.*

Fruit: The Christ was the Author and Finisher of the example of Who we need to follow after, to run this race. We are to put away every weight, the world, and anything that causes us to quit the race for Him. Jesus didn't quit when He walked the earth. He fulfilled His purpose for our Father, and for us; so that we may receive salvation, and God's grace & mercy.

No matter how hard it may seem, we will never have it as hard as Jesus did. But we are to continue running this race, for ourselves, and others. And though it may seem that no one is listening, some are. God has put in each one of us a gift, and that gift is purposed for someone or some people that we will cross paths with. It will be a Blessing to them.

Galatians 6:9 ESV: And let us not grow weary of doing good, for in due season we will reap, if we do not give up.

Just as The Christ is now seated at the right hand of our Father, we will be with them as well, if we do not give up, and grow weary of doing good. There is nothing better than for us to reap a reward of living in Paradise with our Lord & Savior! Where a day is forever! Time is not kept in Heaven!

The Apostle Paul says to Timothy in a letter, **2 Timothy 4:7-8 ESV:** I have fought the good fight, I have finished the race, I have kept the faith. Henceforth there is laid up for me the crown of righteousness, which the Lord, the righteous judge, will award to me on that Day, and not only to me but also to all who have loved his appearing.

We will also receive the crown of righteousness by running this race for Him!

Be Blessed!!!

YOUR FRUIT

Day 34 – Infinite Forgiveness

Good Morning my Beautiful Sunshines!

Seed: Our Spiritual Food for Today, comes from: ***Ephesians 1:7 ESV: In him we have redemption through his blood, the forgiveness of our trespasses, according to the riches of his grace,***

Fruit: Wow, that is a lot of forgiveness! Only by His grace that will never cease, while we are on this side.

But who could only bring about redemption and God's amazing grace, when we accept our Lord & Savior and ask for forgiveness of our sins? Only One! Jesus, sweet Jesus! The Holy Lamb!

It was the most unselfish act of the love of Jesus to please our Father, that has ushered in God's forgiveness of our sins. Each time we go to Him with a sincere and humbled heart. Jesus then takes our prayers, and rocks it in His bosom and presents it to our Father! And our Father is just to forgive us for our sins.

God cannot go back on His Word. If that were so, Jesus would have died in vain, and that would make God a liar. And we know that He is not a liar, nor did our Savior bear the cross without purpose.

Let's learn to forgive others, just as God forgives us! Infinite forgiveness!

Be Blessed!!!

YOUR FRUIT

Day 35 – Live For The One Who Gave Us Life

Good Morning my Beautiful Sunshines!

Seed: Our Spiritual Food for Today, comes from: *2 Corinthians 5:14-15 ESV: For the love of Christ controls us, because we have concluded this: that one has died for all, therefore all have died; and he died for all, that those who live might no longer live for themselves but for him who for their sake died and was raised.*

Fruit: If we say we love Jesus, that love for Him should constrain us from making this life all about us! He didn't bear that cross for a select few, or just for me, but for all!

Of course, God wants you to live a Blessed, prosperous, and loving life; in harmony with each other, but first with Him!

No one but Jesus could have paid the ransom for our sins. This is why we put Him before us! Glorifying and praising Him, and not ourselves nor anyone else! Worshiping Him in spirit and in truth, and not worshiping man, or things!

When we get our priorities straight, He will Bless us with the desires of our hearts! Seek Him, and His Kingdom first!

And just in case you are wondering or perceive others as being "blessed" with things, and you see them doing all kinds of things that is not of God; remember you don't know what they do to get those things, or who they worship, what they went thru to get what they have.

So never think God has forgotten about your faithfulness! It just takes patience, endurance, and faith!

Remember Job!

Be Blessed!!!

YOUR FRUIT

Day 36 – Are We Not Our Sisters and Brothers Keepers?

Good Morning my Beautiful Sunshines!

Seed: Our Spiritual Food for Today, comes from: *1 John 3:16-17 ESV: By this we know love, that he laid down his life for us, and we ought to lay down our lives for the brothers. But if anyone has the world's goods and sees his brother in need, yet closes his heart against him, how does God's love abide in him?*

Fruit: Ouch! Yet we say we love our Lord & Savior because He gave His life for our sins. How can we say we love Him? When our fellow brothers and sisters are lacking in a many things, and when God has Blessed so many of us with more than we will ever need!

We will spend our money on lavish parties, clothes that we will never wear, shoes that we will never wear, purses we will never carry, cars that we will hardly drive, and a host of other worldly things we will never fully enjoy. Because we have too much.

Some of us will see a homeless person on the street, or a coworker that doesn't have money for lunch, nothing to eat, and we will look the other way. I know, it's not our problem. That's a lie, and if we think this way, the truth is not in us. And the truth is Jesus.

We are to be our brothers and sisters keepers, and if necessary, lay down our lives for them.

Jesus died for our sins, and He also wants us to be just like Him!

How can we say we love the Father, Whom we never seen, and not show love and compassion to our brothers and sisters, whom we see daily?

Be Blessed!!!

YOUR FRUIT

Day 37 – Jesus Has The Power

Good Morning my Beautiful Sunshines!

Seed: Our Spiritual Food for Today, comes from: ***Matthew 28:18 ESV: And Jesus came and said to them, "All authority in heaven and on earth has been given to me.***

Fruit: Spread the good news of The Gospel of our Father!

The enemy doesn't want us to know this. He wants us to think he has the power. And what power he has, Jesus allows him to have. Don't think for one second that all the things that go on in the world, takes God by surprise. And you can read ***Ecclesiastes 1:9-10 ESV***, which will clearly confirm this.

When God is ready to set order, He will. But know His will, shall be done. And since I believe Scripture to be God's Truth, the world will not get better. He will give the enemy reign for a little while, but when it's time, IT'S TIME!

We as believers just need to pray without ceasing, and armor ourselves with The Word of God.

Jesus was obedient to the very end, and has been given power and dominion over everything! I would rather follow The One with the power in Heaven, and on earth. Than the one who has been given temporary reign, to further his own demise, and his followers.

Be Blessed!!!

YOUR FRUIT

Day 38– A Perfect Living Example

Good Morning my Beautiful Sunshines!

Seed: Our Spiritual Food for Today, comes from: *Hebrews 1:3 ESV: He is the radiance of the glory of God and the exact imprint of his nature, and he upholds the universe by the word of his power. After making purification for sins, he sat down at the right hand of the Majesty on high,*

Fruit: Being that Jesus was the only one to fulfill our Father's desire. He had to fashion Himself a fleshly body to get this major task done.

Jesus didn't just talk, teach, and preach about The Word, He upheld The Word, by being a living example.

I know we've all heard from our parents, "Do as I say, and not as I do." Sorry, that dog don't hunt.

We are what shapes, and mold our children's characteristics by what they hear us say, and see what we do. This is why Jesus lived by His words, and didn't just talk to His Disciples without actions behind His words, nor the multitude of people He ministered to.

When we practice what we preach, and live by what we tell our children, we would have some God fearing, and loving children. And they would receive such praises and rewards from us.

This is why Jesus now sits at the right hand of our Father, because He fulfilled our Father's purpose, without error, and by being a living example of who our Father is!

Be Blessed!!!

YOUR FRUIT

Day 39 – Live As Christ

Good Morning my Beautiful Sunshines!

Seed: Our Spiritual Food for Today, comes from: *Romans 5:6-8 ESV: For while we were still weak, at the right time Christ died for the ungodly. For one will scarcely die for a righteous person—though perhaps for a good person one would dare even to die— but God shows his love for us in that while we were still sinners, Christ died for us.*

Fruit: Because we didn't have a leg to stand on, we were bound for hell! God was fed up with our actions, and not a one could save our souls, so He sent Jesus, The Holy Lamb to be crucified, for our ungodliness! No one could seem to get it right.

Some of us, perhaps may die for a good cause, or our children, a "righteous" person perhaps? Love of country? But who we are/were didn't matter to Jesus. While we are yet still sinners, He died for us all!

Although, we can never repay The Christ for His sacrifice, we can strive to live as He lived on this side.

Aren't you glad that Jesus have that unconditional love? I know I am. Even in our unrighteousness, He is yet still compassionate toward us. Even those that persecuted Him.

I am still in awe, as to His inconceivable love, and forgiveness. Just amazing to me.

Be Blessed!!!

YOUR FRUIT

Day 40 – Vengeance Is The Lord's

Good Morning my Beautiful Sunshines!

Seed: Our Spiritual Food for Today, comes from: ***Romans 12:19 ESV Beloved, never avenge yourselves, but leave it to the wrath of God, for it is written, "Vengeance is mine, I will repay, says the Lord."***

Fruit: On my way to work one morning, I was listening to Deitrick Haddon's song, titled "Stand Still", and guest Artist, Pastor Donnie McClurkin.

Let me give you a little bit of it. "Your enemies know not what they do, when they declare war on you, you think by now they would have figured out, The Lord will always see you thru."

And this is The Truth! God say's, "Vengeance is Mine, I will repay", and with that being said.

I know sometimes when we are hurt by the ones we love, by a family member, friend, or someone we are in a relationship with; we want to get them back. But move out the way, DO NOT take matters into your own hands. God has already worked that out.

And when He does, you will have to pray to our Father to please ease up off of them.

God don't like for anybody to mistreat, use, and abuse His children. So, it's not our battle, it's The Lord's! Just move out the way!

Please, please, please think before you react! It is the trick of the enemy, and you will end up bound in their chains!

Let it go, and get in The Word! It's the only thing that will give you peace, joy, happiness, and love. Although not an overnight process; but with all things, they work according to God's will, and purpose.

Life is too short for anyone to consume your mind with wanting to seek revenge! They are not worth it, and you are blocking what God wants to give you! Someone far better!

Be Blessed!!!

YOUR FRUIT

Day 41 – Jesus Overcame, and So Can We

Good Morning my Beautiful Sunshines!

Seed: Our Spiritual Food for Today, comes from: *1 Peter 2:24 ESV: He himself bore our sins in his body on the tree, that we might die to sin and live to righteousness. By his wounds you have been healed.*

Fruit: Yes, we "should" live into righteousness for what Jesus did for us. I can hear Him say, "I am doing this for you, and all you have to do is live by God's Word, acknowledge who I am, be baptized, and The Comforter is gifted unto you, to be your guide."

"And if by chance you should stumble and fall down, I died and took all those stripes for you to ask for forgiveness, Repent, and turn from that sin. Give that sin a name, so you can overcome it."

We should not take advantage of our Holy Lamb's sacrifice! Just know that The Christ has not, and will not ever ask us to do something He hasn't done already, nor overcame!

He tells us in *John 16:33 ESV: I have said these things to you, that in me you may have peace. In the world you will have tribulation. But take heart; I have overcome the world."*

Surely, if He overcame the world, we can give it our best effort to run this race, and give our gratitude for His sacrifice for us.

The road won't be easy, but with Him in the mist. He will carry us.

Be Blessed!!!

YOUR FRUIT

Day 42 – Be Anxious For Nothing

Good Morning my Beautiful Sunshines!

Seed: Our Spiritual Food for Today, comes from: *Matthew 6:25, 30 ESV: "Therefore I tell you, do not be anxious about your life, what you will eat or what you will drink, nor about your body, what you will put on. Is not life more than food, and the body more than clothing? But if God so clothes the grass of the field, which today is alive and tomorrow is thrown into the oven, will he not much more clothe you, O you of little faith?*

Fruit: Now faith! Let me say that again! Now faith!

God's children will never have to worry about going hungry, thirsty, being clothed, nor having a place to live; none of that!

We may say, but I have been without. Where was God then? It wasn't God, He never leaves us, we leave Him. It was our lack of faith in Him. And yes, our disobedience.

God isn't telling us to go out and buy name brand clothing for our tots, when we have rent to pay. He doesn't tell us to spend our money on cell phones with all the latest technology, and neglect putting food in our refrigerator. That would be us, and we really need to examine ourselves and know that God does supply our needs. You have to seek Him first and His kingdom in order for Him to give you some of the desires of your heart, without it being a burden on your finances.

God draws near to those who draw near to Him! We have to invite Him into your life. We have to be obedient to God's Word. We can't expect God to take care of our needs, and wants when we are living any kind of way! For *Psalms 37:3-4 ESV :* says, *Trust in the LORD, and do good; dwell in the land and befriend faithfulness. Delight yourself in the LORD, and he will give you the desires of your heart.*

Let's exercise our faith and practice obedience and self-control, so that God will fulfill our needs. Be mindful to do what He ask us to do, and He will work it all out!

Be Blessed!!!

YOUR FRUIT

Day 43 – All Have Sinned, But We Are Not To Stay In It

Good Morning my Beautiful Sunshines!

Seed: Our Spiritual Food for Today, comes from: ***Romans 3:23-24 ESV: for all have sinned and fall short of the glory of God, and are justified by his grace as a gift, through the redemption that is in Christ Jesus,***

Fruit: Meaning only one was perfect, and perfected living life on this side. So, with that said, none of us are perfect, and have no heaven or hell to put anyone in.

And we have to be mindful not to be the judge and jury for others. When we line up with The Word, others will see Christ in us, and eventually they will begin their transformation.

However, some will have you believe that we can continue in sin, and live a sinful life, and expect to still live out eternity in Heaven. And we need to get the enemy out our ear, for those who want to believe this.

Consider ***Romans 6:1-2 ESV: What shall we say then? Are we to continue in sin that grace may abound? By no means! How can we who died to sin still live in it?***

So once we accept Jesus as our Lord and Savior; we are saying we are putting away those sinful things we use to do. We are saying, we are now going to live Christ like. We are saying we will deny the lust of our flesh! We are saying that we will put on the whole armor of Christ, and run this race just as He did!

So please do not let anyone tell you it is ok to continue to sin and expect to get into Heaven.

God cannot stand sin, and if He had to turn away from His only Begotten Son when He bore the sins of the world on that cross, surely we don't expect God to do anything different!

Be Blessed!!!

YOUR FRUIT

Day 44 – Seek God's Approval

Good Morning my Beautiful Sunshines!

Seed: Our Spiritual Food for Today, comes from: *Romans 13:8 ESV: Owe no one anything, except to love each other, for the one who loves another has fulfilled the law.*

I will also give you *Psalms 37:21 ESV: The wicked borrows but does not pay back, but the righteous is generous and gives;*

Also, *Matthew 6:12 ESV: and forgive us our debts, as we also have forgiven our debtors.*

Fruit: Our Father wants us to live debt free. Not owing anyone, anything. When we owe someone, it can cause issues, if we do not repay our debtor back, we become prisoners to them; especially a family member. And this leads to all kind of confusion, and dislike for the borrower, because we know they have the money to pay us back, but they take us for granted and feel like we don't need our money back.

We see them in the mall, nail shop, hair salon, going out to eat, at the club, and knowing they owe us. And they will avoid us like the plague. Now this is what the scripture calls a wicked borrower. They have no intentions of paying us back.

But we are to love and forgive our debtors anyway! Scriptures clearly says, love fulfilled the law, and love is a commandment.

Also consider *Luke 14:28 ESV: For which of you, desiring to build a tower, does not first sit down and count the cost, whether he has enough to complete it?* Now we know this is some of us. Talking to myself! We don't care how much that car, house, or trip cost us; we just know we want it. Forget what God say! We will forget other bills, sell blood, our bodies, just to have those worldly things, knowing good and well we can't afford them.

This is why *Matthew 6:33 ESV:* says, *But seek first the kingdom of God and his righteousness, and all these things will be added to you.*

Be Blessed!!!

YOUR FRUIT

Day 45 – There Is Power In His Name

Good Morning my Beautiful Sunshines!

Seed: Our Spiritual Food for Today, comes from: *1 Corinthians 1:18 ESV: For the word of the cross is folly to those who are perishing, but to us who are being saved it is the power of God.*

Fruit: The unbelievers talk foolishness about what our Lord & Savior, about God, about religion. They can't comprehend that Jesus fashioned Himself a physical body, and would die for people like us. And if we believe in Him there is this place that is better than earth. Not giving honor to Jesus for gifting unto us the most greatest gift that man has ever been given, is pretty much suicide.

The only reason their finite minds can come up with is, they were not there to witness it, and there is nobody that existed that healed the sick, raised the dead, and gave sight to the blind, so it's hard for the unbeliever to comprehend! They ask; "Where is the evidence?"

What does *Hebrews 11:1 ESV* say? *Now faith is the assurance of things hoped for, the conviction of things not seen.*

Our faith, as believers does not allow us to think foolishness! We know the feeling we get, by just calling Jesus name! Try it, and see if you don't get chills all over your body!

There is so much power in the name of Jesus! Scripture says the demons tremble, *James 2:19 ESV.*

As Believers we know Jesus as our Savior, our way Maker, our Mediator, our Convictor, our Intercessor, our Comfort, our Joy, our Peace, our Healer, Jesus is our everything!

There is no one like Him! So I know, without a shadow of a doubt; it all comes back to the cross, and His resurrection. The sacrifice He made to save a sin sick dying world, and that was all by God's power!

Be Blessed!!!

YOUR FRUIT

Day 46 – Pray For Our Sisters and Brothers

Good Morning my Beautiful Sunshines!

Seed: Our Spiritual Food for Today, comes from: **Luke 22:31-32 ESV: *"Simon, Simon, behold, Satan demanded to have you, that he might sift you like wheat, but I have prayed for you that your faith may not fail. And when you have turned again, strengthen your brothers."***

Fruit: This is a good one! It's almost like I can feel Jesus words!

Jesus knew that Peter was about to be tested like never before! Peter was a militant, outspoken, and very confident.

Peter thought he would be willing to die with Jesus, but Jesus knew what Peter was going to do. Peter denied Jesus 3 times. What hurt and shame Peter must have felt, after denying Jesus! He didn't feel worthy of Jesus love anymore.

But remember Jesus told Peter, "I've already prayed. After you forgive yourself and find strength in Me, then strengthen your brothers and sisters."

We should take comfort of knowing that someone has/is already praying for us. We may feel as though we can take on the world. And we learn that some battles are not to be fought, we will find ourselves as Peter did. We will feel hurt, and shame because we will see ourselves as a failure.

Just as a drug addict, when they have gotten off drugs for a period of time. Start reading The Word, and going to fellowship with other sisters and brothers in Christ. They may feel as though they are strong enough to hang around those friends they use to get high with. But, the enemy will do everything he can, in order for an addict to start using again. Often times, someone will offer to get that recovering addict high, for free. The addict will turn the offer down a couple of times, but if the addict continues to be in that environment, eventually he/she will succumb to those temptations. And after the first hit, he/she will feel like a failure.

We are to pray for our fellow sisters and brothers who have fallen, actually before they fall. When we stop feeding our spirit man, we grow weak to the world, and have no defense to fight off temptations.

We are to help them get back up! It is our duty!

Be Blessed!!!

YOUR FRUIT

Day 47 – The Spiritual Heart

Good Morning my Beautiful Sunshines!

Seed: Our Spiritual Food for Today comes from: ***Romans 10:9-10 ESV: because, if you confess with your mouth that Jesus is Lord and believe in your heart that God raised him from the dead, you will be saved. For with the heart one believes and is justified, and with the mouth one confesses and is saved.***

Fruit: This is great news! Call on the name of sweet Jesus with our mouth, but we can't just call that name any kind of way! We have to believe with our hearts.

Once it penetrates our heart, which is in the pit of our bowels, it gets spiritual, and we become transformed into a new creation.

The heart, it is the most important organ in our body! Without our heart, we can't survive.

With our heart, we feel it, and we confess it with our mouth that God raised our Lord & Savior, Jesus from the dead.

You ever been in love? And you tell that person you love them with all your heart! And the other person believes this, because they feel that love with their heart! That love is deeper than the physical heart, it's the love that has attached itself to your soul! That's why you both can complete each other's sentences. You know when they are in pain, when they are happy. When something is bothering them.

This is the kind of heart belief our Father is referring to!

God knows when we pray and confess with our hearts that it's genuine. He can feel it! This is when He starts to draw near to us, because now we truly believe!

Be Blessed!!!

YOUR FRUIT

Day 48 – Study For Yourself

Good Morning my Beautiful Sunshines!

Seed: Our Spiritual Food for Today comes from: *2 Timothy 2:15 ESV: Do your best to present yourself to God as one approved, a worker who has no need to be ashamed, rightly handling the word of truth.*

Fruit: Don't just take someone's word about what God Word says, nor mine! Scripture says, study to show thyself approve.

If we live our lives based off what we are told, i.e. "It's ok to do this and that, you don't have to do anything but call on the name of Jesus and live as you are". And this LIE caused you to be misguided, well.... Let's just say, you will be in for a rude awakening. Literally, when you go before our Father, when we get to the other side! Oh, and they will also!

If you truly believe you can live this life any kind of wretched way, by all means go ahead!

Study God's Word! And don't allow the words of LIES, IGNORANCE, and interpretation of someone else become that determining factor of you having to leave Heaven, and not receive the crown of righteousness. Especially, when their actions, nor teaching do not line up with The Word of God.

But how would you know, if you don't study The Word for yourself?

If we listen to false doctrine and we become teachers and preachers, using the same false doctrine; we are bringing about damnation to ourselves, and others.

Study The Word for yourself, and do not be ashamed to ask questions when someone wants to come alone and try and teach you anything else, other than The Word of God.

Be Blessed!!!

YOUR FRUIT

Day 49 – For God's Glory

Good Morning my Beautiful Sunshines!

Seed: Our Spiritual Food for Today, comes from: *1 Corinthians 3:4-8 ESV: For when one says, "I follow Paul," and another, "I follow Apollos," are you not being merely human? What then is Apollos? What is Paul? Servants through whom you believed, as the Lord assigned to each. I planted, Apollos watered, but God gave the growth. So neither he who plants nor he who waters is anything, but only God who gives the growth. He who plants and he who waters are one, and each will receive his wages according to his labor.*

Fruit: The Apostle Paul is laying it down in this letter. He is letting the church of Corinth know that although the method of the teaching is different, the message is the same. The Gospel of God!

For one teacher may plant God's Word in you. Another teacher comes alone, and their purpose is to cultivate The Word of God in you. God has given you the increase by your hearing, studying, applying, and laboring in His Ministry.

In ministry, it shouldn't matter what position we hold, we should all be working for His Glory! One can be the president of the usher board, and one can be an usher. But if the president have a bad attitude and are never on time for a meeting, the usher is always greeting the church with a smile, and always on time for every meeting. Who's reward will be greater? Of course, the usher!

You see, it doesn't matter what position we hold in God's Ministry. As long as we are working in our gifting. And if we do it diligently, for God's Glory and not our own, He will increase us!

This is why it is very important that we are working in our gifting. And if we don't know what gift(s) God gave us, ask Him, and He will reveal it to us.

Be Blessed!!!

YOUR FRUIT

Day 50 – Death Has No Sting in Christ Jesus

Good Morning my Beautiful Sunshines!

Seed: Our Spiritual Food for Today, comes from: *1 Corinthians 15:55-57 ESV: "O death, where is your victory? O death, where is your sting?" The sting of death is sin, and the power of sin is the law. But thanks be to God, who gives us the victory through our Lord Jesus Christ.*

I'm going to also give you *1 Corinthians 15:50 ESV: I tell you this, brothers: flesh and blood cannot inherit the kingdom of God, nor does the perishable inherit the imperishable.*

Fruit: Just as water and oil don't mix, neither do the spirit and the flesh mix. The flesh cannot survive in the heavenly realm.

We also know that our flesh is weak, and the flesh is the reason we sin daily! We must live in the spirit, and deny our flesh daily to live in the spirit.

The only way death will have a sting, and the grave will have victory over us, is up to us, and how we choose to live our lives on this side! We can either gird up, and put on the whole armor of Christ and live Christ like (in the spirit), or we can continually live in the lust of our flesh (self-righteous, envy, jealousy, strive, hatred, heresies, and etc.) **Galatians 5:19-21.**

Thanks be to God, for allowing His only Begotten Son, Jesus to show us how to take away the sting of death, and the victory of the grave.

Let's all strive to live as Christ on this side, so that we can all be together in our Father's House forever, worshipping and praising Him together. In our new spiritual bodies, on the other side.

Be Blessed!!!

YOUR FRUIT

Day 51 – Every Knee Shall Bow

Good Morning my Beautiful Sunshines!

Seed: Our Spiritual Food for Today, comes from: *Romans 14:11 ESV: for it is written, "As I live, says the Lord, every knee shall bow to me, and every tongue shall confess to God."*

Fruit: Jesus didn't say, every knee may bow, should bow; nor did He say every tongue may confess, should confess, He said "SHALL BOW, and CONFESS!"

Meaning we don't or will not have a say so in the matter of bowing, and confessing to our Father that Jesus is Lord!

We all have to go before Him and confess to Him the good, the bad, and the ugly! For He will be our Judge!

I don't know about you, but I believe that He is Lord. He is Alpha and Omega, The Creator of everything!

I will strive to be a good servant, and live my life on this side as He commands us all to do! I have personally experienced His wrath a many of times, so I know who He is, and what He will do, when we are disobedient! I have experienced His grace, mercy, and Blessings. And I know that He loves us so much!

There is no greater love than God's love! No, not a one!

If you can just see what I see, feel what I feel, and you will know without a shadow of a doubt, that HE IS REAL!!!

Love God and others, the way He loves you and I! Go to Him, with a sincere heart, and let Him show you who He is! Release everything to Him, and allow Him to work everything out for you!

After you experience His greatness, you will want to bow and confess on this side, that HE IS LORD! No longer will you wait until you get on the other side.

Be Blessed!!!

YOUR FRUIT

Day 52 – Cleansed By His Blood

Good Morning my Beautiful Sunshines!

Seed: Our Spiritual Food for Today, comes from: *1 Peter 1:18-19 ESV: knowing that you were ransomed from the futile ways inherited from your forefathers, not with perishable things such as silver or gold, but with the precious blood of Christ, like that of a lamb without blemish or spot.*

Fruit: There is a song that says, "I'd rather have Jesus, than silver and gold".

God couldn't use things that will perish for our ransom. It took One, that was without spot or blemish. It took Jesus to pay our ransom, from the wrath of our Father.

Not even our forefathers were worthy enough to pay our ransom, and many were great men. God used them in many wonderful ways, but yet, they still sinned. And because they sinned, we inherited those futile (fruitless) ways as well.

We can now be assured that we can all bear good fruit. And the choice is ours; which is by living as Jesus lived, accepting Him as our Lord & Savior, and inhabiting the fruits of The Holy Spirit.

Allowing The Christ to wash away our sins, with His precious and Holy Blood.

We are not to take the precious Blood of Jesus lightly, nor for granted. Remembering that it was Him, that could only pay such a debt, so that we can stand a chance to be in a right relationship with our Father in Heaven.

It wouldn't hurt to Thank Him daily for what He has done for us. Jesus didn't have to descend, nor stay on that cross, but it was our Father's desire for Him to save His children from His wrath.

And we should Thank Jesus for His obedience, and sacrifice.

Be Blessed!!

YOUR FRUIT

Day 53 – We Are To Represent The Christ

Good Morning my Beautiful Sunshines!

Seed: Our Spiritual Food for Today, comes from: *Colossians 1:27-28 ESV: To them God chose to make known how great among the Gentiles are the riches of the glory of this mystery, which is Christ in you, the hope of glory. Him we proclaim, warning everyone and teaching everyone with all wisdom, that we may present everyone mature in Christ.*

Fruit: The Christ is our hope of glory! Hidden from many, because of the blinds they have on. Now as Gentiles, we are also joint heirs to receive the same Glory!

To those whom God has called to preach and teach, it is our obligation to make sure we are not compromising, or watering down The Word. If we do not represent The Christ in spirit and in truth, it could cause many to stumble and fall. And we will be held accountable!

It is our duty, and our purpose to those who have been called, to spread the good news of The Gospel. Making disciples out of those who do not know God in the pardon of their sins. This is a commandment Jesus gave to the 11 disciples, in **Matthew 28:19-20 ESV:** *Go therefore and make disciples of all nations, baptizing them in the name of the Father and of the Son and of the Holy Spirit, teaching them to observe all that I have commanded you. And behold, I am with you always, to the end of the age."*

And as long as this is what Jesus commands, we should know that He is with us, and will be our guide.

This is why it is so important that we remove ourselves when we are teaching, and preaching The Gospel. We may become self-righteous, and the need to be self-gratified, and not glorifying our Father.

Speaking the truth will never harm anyone, it's the lies and deceit that does us harm!

Be Blessed!!!

YOUR FRUIT

Day 54 – Jesus Gives New Life

Good Morning my Beautiful Sunshines!

Seed: Our Spiritual Food for Today, comes from: *Hebrews 7:25 ESV: Consequently, he is able to save to the uttermost those who draw near to God through him, since he always lives to make intercession for them.*

Fruit: This simply means, it doesn't matter how far we have sunk, how low we have become; Jesus will accept us when we go to Him!

Man/woman may not accept us, or like us when we are in the gutter, but our Lord & Savior, Jesus certainly will!

He is here for us, just for the asking! If you feel like you are to engulfed with sin and don't feel like you are worthy of God's love, well, that is only the enemy deceiving you! Get him out your ear!

Does not the scripture say in *Matthew 11:28-30 ESV: Come to me, all who labor and are heavy laden, and I will give you rest. Take my yoke upon you, and learn from me, for I am gentle and lowly in heart, and you will find rest for your souls. For my yoke is easy, and my burden is light."*

Jesus is always here for everyone, Who better than to give all of our struggles, troubles, and situations to Him, when they get too tough for us?

We don't have to wait until we feel as though we need to get our lives straightened out. Perhaps, this is the problem. When we try and straighten our situations out, we end up making the situation worse.

We need to come to Him as we are, and allow Him to straighten our troubles and situations out. This is what He does! Minister to the sick, He revives us, and gives us a new life.

There is nothing in this world, too hard for God! Nothing! Give it to Him, and trust Him at His Word!

Be Blessed!!!

YOUR FRUIT

Day 55 – Restoring The Lost

Good Morning my Beautiful Sunshines!

Seed: Our Spiritual Food for Today, comes from: *Luke 19:10 ESV: For the Son of Man came to seek and to save the lost."*

Fruit: This was Jesus mission when He fashioned Himself a physical body! He came to seek the sick, and minister to their hearts. To call everyone to repentance, that they may receive the crown of life, on the other side.

Now it is our turn to seek Him out, learn from Him, and trust Him at His word. To build our lives in and thru Him! A solid foundation that will withstand anything that may come up against us.

I had someone communicate to me, they needed to get their life in order before they came to Church. Really? And when might this happen?

Jesus doesn't care about our lives being in order before coming to Him. Again, He came to save the lost. This is one of the reasons His Churches were established.

We are to establish that spiritual relationship with our Father, so that He may pour into us what He needs to, in order for us to be workers in His vineyard.

So on that day He calls us home, and receive us in His bosom! We want to hear Him say as in *Matthew 25:23 ESV: His master said to him, 'Well done, good and faithful servant. You have been faithful over a little; I will set you over much. Enter into the joy of your master.'*

Nothing but joy in the Lord, and His House!

Be Blessed!!!

YOUR FRUIT

Day 56 – A Renewed Mind and Right Spirit

Good Morning my Beautiful Sunshines!

Seed: Our Spiritual Food for Today, comes from: *Romans 12:2 ESV: Do not be conformed to this world, but be transformed by the renewal of your mind, that by testing you may discern what is the will of God, what is good and acceptable and perfect.*

Fruit: Same actions and way of thinking, will surely give you the same results!

How is it that we will accept The Christ as our Lord & Savior, and still continue in the things we did, before accepting Him, and asking Him to come into our lives?

It is understood that change does not come about over night, but it shouldn't take us a year to show some form of growth in our walk with Him. When we accept The Christ as our Lord & Savior, we must put into action that what we are submitting to. Which is His will and His way.

Actions require us to do something. We must study His Word, so that we learn who He is, how we must conduct ourselves, learn to identify what His will is for us, we must pray, meditate, and do those things which will put us in a different mindset. And staying in the old, will not transform us, nor renew our minds.

It is the only way that God will reveal His secrets to us, so that we can fulfill our purpose for Him.

Be Blessed!!!

YOUR FRUIT

Day 57 – Do Not Allow The Enemy To Rob You

Good Morning my Beautiful Sunshines!

Seed: Our Spiritual Food for Today comes from: *Ephesians 4:14-16 ESV: so that we may no longer be children, tossed to and fro by the waves and carried about by every wind of doctrine, by human cunning, by craftiness in deceitful schemes. Rather, speaking the truth in love, we are to grow up in every way into him who is the head, into Christ, from whom the whole body, joined and held together by every joint with which it is equipped, when each part is working properly, makes the body grow so that it builds itself up in love.*

Fruit: As God's children we should know better than to allow man/woman to feed our spirits with any kind of doctrine! And many are really deceived, as some of us want to believe we can do anything, live any kind of way, and still live in Heaven forever, after we leave this side.

Some will tell you God doesn't exist and they have the proof. Really? That's when we say, "Get thee behind me satan!"

Remember satan is a fallen angel and 1/3 of the angels fell with him! Naturally, the enemy will do anything to try and deceive us!

When we know the truth, study the truth, and hear the truth; the Word grows in us with both heart and head knowledge. When we are equipped with the living Word, we cannot be tossed to and fro with any doctrine! We know when someone is talking be-foolery to us! That is, if we are studying the Word, and want to take the path less traveled! That road is narrow, and have some growing pains!

This is why many are deceived, they don't like to be obedient to God's Word. And seemed to think, it is no fun to live by His Word.

But what's so hard about loving our Father with our whole heart, mind and soul, and loving one another? What is so hard about abstaining from sex until being married? What is so hard about only loving one spouse, and not fornicating with many partners? What's so hard about not stealing, and lying? What's so hard about obeying our parents? What's so hard about being our sisters and brothers keepers? And so on, and so on.

Think about it. If we were obedient to God, we would be some of the joyful and most peaceful people. And it's because He would be in the mist, ensuring we have what we need, and the desires of our heart.

The more we study and apply the Word, the more we become Like Christ! And this brings about what God designed us to do! There is nothing wasted, and all is effectively working for His glory, through us!

Be Blessed!!!

YOUR FRUIT

_____

_____

_____

_____

_____

_____

_____

_____

_____

_____

_____

_____

_____

_____

_____

Day 58 – Our Faith Gets God To Move

Good Morning my Beautiful Sunshines!

Seed: Our Spiritual Food for Today, comes from: *Hebrews 11:6 ESV: And without faith it is impossible to please him, for whoever would draw near to God must believe that he exists and that he rewards those who seek him.*

Fruit: Now we profess with our mouth and believe in our hearts that Jesus died on that old rugged cross, although we were not there, our faith and The Gospel tells us He did!

Without faith it won't please God, because when we have doubt, it is saying to God, we are not sure that Jesus died on the cross. When everything that we do, all goes back to the cross! His death was the remission for our sins. And each day when we ask for forgiveness of our daily sins, they are nailed to the cross.

So if we don't believe and have faith that God can't bring us thru any situation, we are saying that our Lord & Savior, Jesus didn't die on that cross.

God knows we have to gain faith, and by this, we have to stay in His Word, pray without ceasing, and allow Him to pour into us what He needs to, to build our faith. And of course, all will not be peaches and cream. It is going to sting a little, and sometimes a lot!

But that's ok, because He has to see us diligently seeking Him to bring us thru, and to totally trust Him!

When we do this! The reward is awesome! There is nothing He won't do for us; for those who love, trust, have faith, and diligently seek Him!

Be Blessed!!!

YOUR FRUIT

Day 59 – Be Careful For What You Pray For

Good Morning my Beautiful Sunshines!

Seed: Our Spiritual Food for Today, comes from: *1 John 5:14-15 ESV: And this is the confidence that we have toward him, that if we ask anything according to his will he hears us. And if we know that he hears us in whatever we ask, we know that we have the requests that we have asked of him.*

Fruit: Often times we ask God for things that are not according to His will, although we may think we should have it/him/her. There are also times when He gives us what we pray for, only to learn it wasn't what we wanted, or needed. He does this to teach us, and to grow us. We will ask, "Lord, why did you allow this to happen? When You knew I didn't need this in my life." And He will say, "Trust Me, it will all work out, I have plans for you. Lean not unto your own understanding. I know it don't feel good right now, but if you put your whole trust in Me, you shall be alright."

Another point about this scripture; some church folks will say they don't want everyone praying for them, because of how they perceive someone to be! I have an issue with this way of thinking! Even if someone is praying for my/your demise, if it's not God's will, it SURELY WILL NOT HAPPEN!!! If you need to read this scripture again, do so! Another scripture that brings this point home is: **Romans 8:31 ESV: What then shall we say to these things? If God is for us, who can be against us?**

Whoever is praying for your demise, may receive it themselves!

I SMH when I hear Christian folks say they don't want everybody praying for them. The one you didn't ask, could be the very prayer God was waiting for, to Bless you! We don't know the relationship they have with God, nor what they are purposed for.

Be Blessed!!!

YOUR FRUIT

Day 60 – A Servant On Fire For The Lord

Good Morning my Beautiful Sunshines!

Seed: Our Spiritual Food for Today, comes from: *Romans 12:10-12 ESV: Love one another with brotherly affection. Outdo one another in showing honor. Do not be slothful in zeal, be fervent in spirit, serve the Lord. Rejoice in hope, be patient in tribulation, be constant in prayer.*

Fruit: Under the influences of The Holy Spirit, He teaches us how to love one another with that brotherly love, as Jesus loves the Church. Honoring one another and ministering to one another.

When we allow The Holy Spirit to take control, and we surrender ourselves to Him, we won't be lazy in doing our Father's business of what we say we were called to do. We can't expect God to show up, when we don't come to choir practice, or ministry meetings on time. When we are practicing praise dancing, or working on fund raisers!

He sees all, and knows all! If we say we have a passion for something, that fervency for God's ministry, there should be no excuse of doing what we need to do, in order for it to be a sweet smelling savor to His nostrils! When we have this zeal, this fire, and passion we are truly and definitely serving Him. It is to magnify and glorify Him only!

Rejoicing in the hope that what we do, will be well pleasing to Him, even when faced with trials and tribulations! Praying for all that He has called us to do, even in the midst of teaching, preaching, singing, praise dancing, and etc.

One can never go wrong with being on fire for The Lord! Sacrificing ourselves and forsaking others in order to truly give Him all we got, in serving Him is never a bad thing!

Be Blessed!!!

YOUR FRUIT

Day 61 – Turn From Sin To Receive God's Favor

Good Morning my Beautiful Sunshines!

Seed: Our Spiritual Food for Today, comes from: *2 Chronicles 7:14 ESV: if my people who are called by my name humble themselves, and pray and seek my face and turn from their wicked ways, then I will hear from heaven and will forgive their sin and heal their land.*

Fruit: This scripture is from God Himself, by the Covenant He made with Israel, and because of their failures under the law. The Israelites began to experience some uneasy times! As they often did!

Some teach that this verse is only meant for the Israelites, and some teach this is for all nations, that if we are disobedient to God, all nations suffer His wrath, when we get out of order.

I agree He was talking to His chosen people, but in my opinion, we can apply it to our nation, as well as our individual lives. Now this is just my opinion, and I'm not trying to lead anyone wrong!

When we say we belong to God, and represent Him, and want a relationship with Him; we will be humble, pray, and seek His face in all things that we do!

No longer then can we continue in our iniquities, wickedness, and expect Him to hear us, heal us, and answer our prayers! We must turn from those things in order for God to forgive us for our sins, and heal whatever it is we are faced with. Whether it be an ailment in the body, our living conditions, relationship, family. Whatever it is. He will answer us, when we humble ourselves, and live according to His will and way.

Be Blessed!!!

YOUR FRUIT

Day 62 – Are You Blessing Others?

Good Morning my Beautiful Sunshines!

Seed: Our Spiritual Food for Today, comes from: ***Proverbs 21:13 ESV: Whoever closes his ear to the cry of the poor will himself call out and not be answered.***

Fruit: When God has Blessed us in abundance, what do we do? Do we keep all those Blessings to ourselves? Do we ever go out and volunteer our time? Do we see a family on the street, and take the long way around just to bypass where they are standing?

I've said on a few occasions, often times God will Bless us to see if we will be a Blessing to others. And if we don't do the right thing. The Lord giveth, and The Lord taketh away!

I'm not just talking about money, or your time. You prayed for a good husband/wife. God answered your prayer, but now that you have a husband/wife, you don't know how to treat him/her. Even a dog get tired of being kicked. So they move on, and you are sitting there asking God why?

Because you didn't do the right thing!

Be Blessed!!!

YOUR FRUIT

Day 63 – Press Forward

Good Morning my Beautiful Sunshines!

Seed: Our Spiritual Food for Today, comes from: *Philippians 3:14 ESV: I press on toward the goal for the prize of the upward call of God in Christ Jesus.*

Fruit: Praise God!!! That He loves us, and He has found us to be testable! The enemy has to send a host of demons for God's believers! Why? I'm glad you ask! Because the enemy knows that we press forward, toward the mark of The Most High!

The enemy knows that we love our Father in Heaven, and with every breath in our bodies, we make every effort to live Christ like! The enemy knows he will get nowhere when he sends them small demons! He has to send a host of them! Yet, and still, we will trust God, and be faithful to Him!

We need to be like The Apostle Paul, and press toward the goal of the prize, and do what God is calling us to do.

Let's pray for one another, that we will not detour, and we will stay the course that of what God has put us on!

For His purpose, and will; and not our own!

Be Blessed!!!

YOUR FRUIT

Day 64 – In The Midst, Rejoice and Pray

Good Morning my Beautiful Sunshines!

Seed: Our Spiritual Food for Today, comes from: *1 Thessalonians 5:16-18 ESV: Rejoice always, pray without ceasing, give thanks in all circumstances; for this is the will of God in Christ Jesus for you.*

Fruit: How can we rejoice evermore and pray without ceasing when we are going thru so much? I'm glad you asked!

It's what the enemy wants us to do! He wants us to be mad at God, and not trust Him at His word! He wants us to wallow in our pity! The enemy wants us bound in depression, our circumstances, bad relationships and etc.! The enemy wants us to believe that God won't bring us thru these issues!

That devil is a liar! That's what the enemy is good at! Lying and deceiving!

How many of you know and believe that when God allows things to happen in our lives, that don't feel good, it is designed and allowed for a reason?

I look at my trials and tribulations as being favored and loved by God! He can't get our attention when all is gravy in our lives. Ask yourself, "Would I really seek God's face when He gives me everything I want? Would I rejoice and pray to Him daily?"

When we get off the path, God has to reel us back in. Those that belong to Him! He requires a relationship with us, and there is something we promised Him we would do for Him. And trust, He will get us back on course, when we get off course.

In spite of what we go thru, trust God, rejoice, and pray without ceasing. If Jesus took all those lashes and the humiliation for sinners like you and I, what makes us think we would not be susceptible to the pain He experienced? If He didn't love us, and want to have a relationship with us, He would just let us live any kind of way!

Be thankful that God wants a relationship with us! It will all work out according to His will and purpose!

Be Blessed!!!

YOUR FRUIT

Day 65 – A Representative of The Christ

Good Morning my Beautiful Sunshines!

Seed: Our Spiritual Food for Today, comes from: *Colossians 4:5-6 ESV: Walk in wisdom toward outsiders, making the best use of the time. Let your speech always be gracious, seasoned with salt, so that you may know how you ought to answer each person.*

Fruit: Ouch! And that was for me! Sometimes I am not so graceful to other believers, and non-believers, when I see some things that are just not true, and misleading!

I have to remember that everyone is not a believer, so I need to be mindful of what I write, and say. I truly don't want to turn away a non-believer, and have them reasoning with themselves, and asking, "Why should I want to be a believer, when this is how Christians act toward one another."

I have to choose my words carefully, and with grace. With good taste, and words that will glorify our Father, and not make Him look bad! I have to represent Him well, where He will be pleased with His daughter.

And if any of you are like me, you have done this also. But let's remember this scripture before we write or say anything to others.

I thank God for this rod of correction! And refrain from getting sucked in by the enemy.

By being graceful and speaking in good taste, we will be walking in wisdom; and those that do not yet believe, will perhaps want to get to know this Jesus that we speak so highly about.

Let's be great representatives of The Christ.

Be Blessed!!!

YOUR FRUIT

Day 66 – Look To The Hills

Good Morning my Beautiful Sunshines!

Seed: Our Spiritual Food for Today, comes from: *Psalm 121:1-2 ESV: I lift up my eyes to the hills. From where does my help come? My help comes from the LORD, who made heaven and earth.*

Fruit: I hear this scripture being recited at funerals often. It is to give encouragement to the bereaved, to let them know, in order to get through such a difficult time of that of a lost one, we can only rely on the help and strength; that will only come from The Lord.

Often times, this scripture can be received with any obstacles we face on this side.

I can recall one Saturday morning where the enemy tried to sift me hard, and he almost had me. The thought of not wanting to go to Church the next morning, crept into my mind. And I didn't feel like praying, but I knew I had to!

But there is Someone GREATER inside me that loves me! I said to myself, "Now this is what the enemy doesn't want me to do, so I'm going to pray and give God the glory, and praise Him in spite of!"

We must realize that what we see and feel in the physical is only a distraction! It is a must for us to know where our help and our strength comes from, when our hearts are heavy.

When we are weary and have heavy hearts, our help and strength doesn't come from man, it comes from The Lord!

Be Blessed!!!

YOUR FRUIT

Day 67 – Walk In The Spirit

Good Morning my Beautiful Sunshines!

Seed: Our Spiritual Food for Today, comes from: *Romans 8:1-2 ESV: There is therefore now no condemnation for those who are in Christ Jesus. For the law of the Spirit of life has set you free in Christ Jesus from the law of sin and death.*

Fruit: Hallelujah! Praise The Lord! For He Is Good!!!

Living and walking in the Spirit is our protection from not being conformed to this world!

What do you mean Bettye? I'm glad you asked!

Living in the spirit, we know where our home will be. We don't allow things, people, hurt, pain to bother us. Sure we have a moment. As our spirits are housed in a fleshly body. But when we realize who we are, what we are here for, and not make this life about us; The Holy Spirit brings to our remembrance that we are only passing thru! Reminding us that we are living for Christ Jesus, and not ourselves!

That when we run this race, and carry that cross, just as our Lord & Savior, Jesus did, we are free indeed! Free from sin! Free from death! Free from life's challenges! Free from burdens! Free from bondage!

We take on a whole new mindset!

And after the flesh has freed our spirits, we spend an eternity with our Father!

Protect yourself, and walk in the spirit of Christ Jesus! It is far greater!

Be Blessed!!!

YOUR FRUIT

Day 68 – Come As You Are

Good Morning my Beautiful Sunshines!

Seed: Our Spiritual Food for Today comes from: *2 Peter 3:9 ESV: The Lord is not slow to fulfill his promise as some count slowness, but is patient toward you, not wishing that any should perish, but that all should reach repentance.*

Fruit: Lord! I know that we take the days you are giving us for granted! Some don't believe you will ever come!

That's some kind of love you are showing us, and we take this Scripture for granted! God doesn't want a soul to perish! Hence the reason why He hasn't showed up, just yet!

His word will go to the 4 corners of the world, and once all have had the opportunity to accept or deny! He Shall return!!!

Each day we open our eyes, do we really think it is going to be our last day?

Do we say, "Oh I will get back with You later, God, ain't nothing going to happen to me."

I wonder how many people have said this, and because they refuse to believe in God, and accept Jesus as their Lord & Savior, now are no longer with us.

It is too late for them, but I can assure you, as long as God gift unto you a new grace and mercy to live another day, there is yet still time for you to accept Jesus, The Christ as your Savior.

Do not be deceived by the enemy. He already know where he is headed, and only wants to take with him as many as he can.

Be Blessed!!!

YOUR FRUIT

Day 69 – God's Way of Settling An Ought

Good Morning my Beautiful Sunshines!

Seed: Our Spiritual Food for Today, comes from: *Matthew 18:15-17 ESV: "If your brother sins against you, go and tell him his fault, between you and him alone. If he listens to you, you have gained your brother. But if he does not listen, take one or two others along with you, that every charge may be established by the evidence of two or three witnesses. If he refuses to listen to them, tell it to the church. And if he refuses to listen even to the church, let him be to you as a Gentile and a tax collector.*

Fruit: As we have seen, many churches don't follow this principle. Most churches want to sweep the most awful behavior of people in the church under a rug, and hope it goes away!

This is the very reason why people do not want to even go to church. They see what goes on in the church, once the ungodly actions have been leaked to the public.

It is also saddening that the people in the church will protect the offender, and cast out the ones that were hurt by the actions of the offender. And because of the cover up, and the majority of the congregation siding with the offender, the offender thinks their actions are ok, and they continue, until the law gets involved, when their actions have offended the law of the land.

There is no repentance in many offenders, as they are not the ones who are being treated like a Gentile, or tax collector, it is the one who was hurt by the offender that is treated in this manner.

However, God does deal with them. And if they are not truly repentance, may The Lord have mercy on them, and their protectors.

Be Blessed!!!

YOUR FRUIT

Day 70 – Hate The Sin, Not The Sinner

Good Morning my Beautiful Sunshines!

Seed: Our Spiritual Food for Today, comes from: *Matthew 7:21-23 ESV: "Not everyone who says to me, 'Lord, Lord,' will enter the kingdom of heaven, but the one who does the will of my Father who is in heaven. On that day many will say to me, 'Lord, Lord, did we not prophesy in your name, and cast out demons in your name, and do many mighty works in your name?' And then will I declare to them, 'I never knew you; depart from me, you workers of lawlessness.'*

Fruit: I stand with Jesus! In that day of reckoning, and when my knees bow before Him. I am reminded and convicted by this:

It is true, I have no heaven or hell to put anyone in! It's very true that God loves us all, however, sin stinks to His nostrils, and He hates sin, but love the sinner.

Bottom line! We know that we fall short, however if there is no admission, there is no remission! And we won't overcome those things that are not pleasing to our Father!

We all have to go before Him for our judgment! And for whoever wants to continue in sin, that's their salvation that is on the line!

Our job as believers is to tell the unchurched, the unbeliever, and nonbeliever about The Christ!

I've learned that we can't make anybody accept Christ, or live by His Word!

God was not, is not, nor will He ever be surprised at what is going on in this world! He is allowing it all to fall in place for the coming of our Lord & Savior, Jesus, The Christ!

All that is going on, has already been predestined, and written!

Yes, we have to do what's not popular! And we may even lose a few friends! My prayer is that what I've written will take root and begin to germinate!

God did give man, his own free will!

The choices we make, depends on us! Good or bad!

We make them, we have to deal with the consequences! Good or bad!

We all tend to forget why Jesus bore that cross!

God was sick of our ways, and sins, almost about to bring upon this world His wrath!

We really have lost sight of Jesus sacrifice!

What will we be told when we get to the other side? Stay, or depart?

Be Blessed!!!

YOUR FRUIT

_____

_____

_____

_____

_____

_____

_____

_____

_____

_____

_____

_____

_____

Day 71 – Free From Bondage

Good Morning my Beautiful Sunshines!

Seed: Our Spiritual Food for Today, comes from: *Ephesians 4:32 ESV: Be kind to one another, tenderhearted, forgiving one another, as God in Christ forgave you.*

Fruit: That's what we must do. Why is it so hard, that not many of us, can be forgiving, kind, and tenderhearted toward one another! And not just a select few, but the whole Body of Christ!

When we go to our Father by way of Jesus being our Mediator, God forgives us. The Christ is there to remind our Father that we have come to Him with a bowed head and a humbled heart, asking for forgiveness of our sins. That He died for our sins, in order for us to confess with our mouths that we recognize and acknowledge the errors of our ways. And we are asking Him for strength to turn from our sins, and disobedience.

When we have sinned against our brother or sister, we go to them and ask for forgiveness, and they should forgive us, and we should do the same, just as God does.

It does none of us any good, when we choose to harbor bitterness, anger, and hatred towards our sisters and brothers. God doesn't want us to be held in bondage, and this is exactly what holds us captive, when we harbor these ungodly characteristics.

We are basically saying we don't want to be free, and we love being in bondage.

Scripture tells us in, *John 8:36 ESV: So if the Son sets you free, you will be free indeed.*

So why not be free! The Son of Man has paid for our freedom, and we shouldn't give it back.

Be Blessed!!!

YOUR FRUIT

Day 72 – Hope and Prayer – Goes Far

Good Morning my Beautiful Sunshines!

Seed: Our Spiritual Food for Today, comes from: *2 Samuel 21:10 ESV: Then Rizpah the daughter of Aiah took sackcloth and spread it for herself on the rock, from the beginning of harvest until rain fell upon them from the heavens. And she did not allow the birds of the air to come upon them by day, or the beasts of the field by night.*

Fruit: Consider Rizpah, a concubine of Saul. Who lost her 2 sons, and they were hanged! "Sometimes Hope Is All We Have!"

Back then sack cloths were used when people were in mourning. They would also put ashes on their head.

Rizpah used that sack cloth to put on a rock during Barley Harvest season to watch over her sons dead bodies. She did this for 5 months with little to no sleep. Guarding her sons to keep the wilds away from salvaging her two son's corpus!

But then David was named king, he saw to it that Rizpah's sons received a proper burial! In your study time, read about Rizpah in its entirety, you should start at **2 Samuel 21:1.**

The message here is, never give up on hope, and prayer! No matter how deem things may look, or become. Our trials and tribulations won't last, when we put our hope and trust in God.

This woman loved her sons so much, even after their spirits had left their body; she went without sleep, bathing, and food; to guard and watch over her sons!

Finally her prayers were answered. This should show us that we may have to wait for quite a while for God to answer our prayers, but we should never lose faith. Once we have prayed, and exercise our faith, God will deliver.

What a great act of love, and endurance!

Be Blessed!!!

YOUR FRUIT

Day 73 – Designed For His Purpose

Good morning my Beautiful Sunshines!

Seed: Our Spiritual Food for Today, comes from: *Psalm 139:13-14 ESV: For you formed my inward parts; you knitted me together in my mother's womb. I praise you, for I am fearfully and wonderfully made. Wonderful are your works; my soul knows it very well.*

Fruit: God has a purpose for us, hence the reason we were born into this world! He crafted us in our mother's wombs, pouring into us His greatness! We were all born with a purpose! If you haven't a clue, seek His face! It was Him that designed you beautifully and wonderfully!

I know some of us don't see the beauty in us, and we question our existence, but if we just stop and not make this life about us, He will reveal those secrets, He has hidden in you! And you will know what your purpose is, on this side.

You can have all the money in the world, and all the material things money can buy; and still fill empty! Why? I'm glad you asked! You haven't sought God's face, to get your assignment! Your reason for living, is for His purpose! Scripture says in **Matthew 6:33 ESV:** *But seek first the kingdom of God and his righteousness, and all these things will be added to you.*

You ever noticed the actions of some wealthy people, and how they can be nasty to others, and you ask yourself, "Why do they act this way, when they are living "The Dream!" This is because they are lonely, empty, and want to make this life about them! Taking no thought on anyone else, only themselves.

But when we realize how great our Father is, and the secrets He poured into us, we will live our life with purpose! With joy, grace, compassion, love, and so many other wonderful characteristics!

Just ask Him, and you shall receive your purposed assignment, on this side!

Be Blessed!!!

YOUR FRUIT

Day 74 – God, In A Class All By Himself

Good Morning my Beautiful Sunshines!

Seed: Our Spiritual Food for Today, comes from: *Ecclesiastes 11:5 ESV: As you do not know the way the spirit comes to the bones in the womb of a woman with child, so you do not know the work of God who makes everything.*

Fruit: We can't even comprehend how our Spirits were created, nor how God, (not evolution) created us in our mother's womb. And we are certainly not on the same thinking level as our Father! Especially when we are not even utilizing a third of our brain. So how could we begin to understand how He created our Spirits, our bodies, and His works?

Scripture says in *1 Corinthians 1:25 ESV: For the foolishness of God is wiser than men, and the weakness of God is stronger than men.*

Even the highest IQ cannot begin to discover God's creation. Many have tried, and many have said, "There must be a higher power." And have been converted to a believer of The One and Only True Living God!

So, instead of questioning how we got here, let's focus on our purpose of what God wants us to do for Him!

We all have gifts that He poured into us, for His purpose! It is by faith that we use those gifts as He would have us to!

As I stated some time ago, if you do not know what your purpose is, just ask our Creator! It shall be revealed to you!

Be Blessed!!!

YOUR FRUIT

Day 75 – Trust God In Spite Of

Good Morning my Beautiful Sunshines!

Seed: Our Spiritual Food for Today, comes from: **Job 1:21 ESV:** *And he said, "Naked I came from my mother's womb, and naked shall I return. The LORD gave, and the LORD has taken away; blessed be the name of the LORD."*

Fruit: Everything that we have, God gifted to us. Those that love Him. We should not be conformed to worldly possessions, as it will corrupt our minds, and could very well cost us our inheritance on the other side.

And if He desires to take the things away from us, He allowed us to have in order to test us, we should still hold faithful to His Word. Should we turn from Him, as Job's wife wanted him to do, God would have known, our love for Him was not sincere, and it was about what He gifted to us.

But if we keep being faithful in spite of our losses, just know that God will Bless us beyond measure, just as He did Job.

This is the reason Job didn't cuss God and die. Job was still faithful and true to God, even after God had allowed everything he possessed to be stripped from him.

Job knew that worldly things didn't matter, and the only thing that matters was to ensure that God was still pleased with his obedience, and that God still loved him.

Besides, all the things we possess on this side, will perish. It is best to serve God, and not things.

Be Blessed!!!

YOUR FRUIT

Day 76 – Godly Conduct Becomes Us

Good Morning my Beautiful Sunshines!

Seed: Our Spiritual Food for Today, comes from: *Zephaniah 3:17 ESV: The LORD your God is in your midst, a mighty one who will save; he will rejoice over you with gladness; he will quiet you by his love; he will exult over you with loud singing.*

Fruit: Remember God is always in the midst of what we are going thru. He is working something mighty in us! Pouring into us, Him! When we learn to trust what He is doing, and allow Him to do His work in us, He rejoices.

We are ready to overcome anything the enemy throws our way. God has equipped us to overcome the wilds of the enemy, not by doing evil for evil, but by His Word, and our conduct. We learn to handle things differently, with love and grace. Ain't nobody mad but the enemy!

There was a time where we would act in a manner that was not of God. When someone did us wrong, but now that we have learned how God wants us to handle these situations, we no longer give anyone the reason to say, "I knew they were a fake Christian".

This gives God great joy when we conduct ourselves in the manner He has taught us.

His love will rest in us! Because He see Himself in us!

The Heaven rejoices when we become, and act godly.

Be Blessed!!!

YOUR FRUIT

Day 77 – No Greater Feeling

Good Morning my Beautiful Sunshines!

Seed: Our Spiritual Food for Today, comes from: *Romans 11:33 ESV: Oh, the depth of the riches and wisdom and knowledge of God! How unsearchable are his judgments and how inscrutable his ways!*

Fruit: We are forever learning in The Gospel of our Father. But how great is that? It is by God's grace to reveal the riches of His wisdom and knowledge!

Scripture says in Deuteronomy 29:29 ESV: "The secret things belong to the LORD our God, but the things that are revealed belong to us and to our children forever, that we may do all the words of this law.

So when we diligently seek Him, He reveals to us, His children, the secrets that was once hidden from us.

It teaches us how He wants us to live our lives! And when His secrets are imputed in our hearts, the wisdom and knowledge He gives to us, is far greater than money, material possessions, diamonds, and pearls!

The Apostle Paul says in *Ephesians 3:8-9 ESV: To me, though I am the very least of all the saints, this grace was given, to preach to the Gentiles the unsearchable riches of Christ, and to bring to light for everyone what is the plan of the mystery hidden for ages in God who created all things,*

Wow, even when we feel like we don't have anything or anyone in this world. Or feel inferior to others based on material wealth, when God reveals His secrets to us, what we have is something that can never ever compare! There is nothing better than to spread and share The Word of God!

Now what greater joy and reward is there, than to share The Word of God, point folks to The Cross, and seeing them come to know Jesus in the pardon of their sins?

It's a huge responsibility! Just goes to show us, that God will use even the least of us, for His will, and purpose!

Be Blessed!!!

YOUR FRUIT

Day 78 – Blessed To Be A Blessing To Others

Good Morning my Beautiful Sunshines!

Seed: Our Spiritual Food for Today, comes from: *Hebrews 6:10 ESV: For God is not unjust so as to overlook your work and the love that you have shown for his name in serving the saints, as you still do.*

Fruit: Our good work, and labor for His glory will not go unappreciated, nor unnoticed by our Father! All that we have poured out to the world, is what God poured in to us.

This scripture reminds me of our Bible Study one night. We touched on Paul, who said, he was now ready to be offered up as a drink offering. Because what God poured into him, and all that He endured. Paul was ready to be offered as a drink offering. He had nothing left, as he was a faithful servant ministering, teaching, and preaching The Word of God to the Gentiles! Paul poured out all that was put into him!

Paul says in, *2 Timothy 4:7 ESV: I have fought the good fight, I have finished the race, I have kept the faith. Henceforth there is laid up for me the crown of righteousness, which the Lord, the righteous judge, will award to me on that Day, and not only to me but also to all who have loved his appearing.*

This should give us comfort to know that we to, will receive the crown of righteousness on the other side; when we have poured out all that God has poured into us, and lived by The Word of God! Even in the midst of trials and tribulations.

Paul knew that his course was about to run out, and Nero had ordered him to the slaughter. This was the last letter he wrote, to Timothy. But he wanted to let Timothy know to keep on running this race, until the very end. He said "his departure is at hand."

Let's stay faithful to our Father, Whom is so worthy, so we to, can receive our crown of righteousness on the other side!

Be Blessed!!!

YOUR FRUIT

Day 79 – God Will Get The Glory

Good Morning my Beautiful Sunshines!

Seed: Our Spiritual Food for Today, comes from: ***Psalm 46:10 KJV: Be still, and know that I am God: I will be exalted among the heathen, I will be exalted in the earth.***

Fruit: God is letting us know that He will get His praise and glory anyway! Whether we do it or not!

If we don't want to praise Him for the many Blessings He has bestowed to us! He says, "It's ok!" God will get the glory, and be exalted whether we do it or not.

If we don't want to give Him glory and honor for bringing us thru, for making a way out of no way, when we know good and well that it was Him, and Him alone that kept His hand on us, and brought us thru some really bad situations! It's ok!

I know many of you have been in some situations, and you wonder, how you ever made it thru, or got out an ordeal alive! I know I have! All I could say was, "But God!"

Many of us want to believe that we are in control of our own destiny, and what you have materially, is because of self, and not God! Just keep believing that! If one truly acquired these things by one's self, wouldn't one be able to keep them? I mean, since some of us believe we are our own god?

But don't think for a minute that the reason we have talents is because of self, nor all that God has gifted to us! God poured something great in to all of us, and He is allowing some of us to use those gifts to see what we are going to do with them.

God says, He will be exalted among folks like this. And in the earth, meaning everywhere! He will get His praises and He will do it Himself!

I know where my Blessings come from! Do you?

God does have a way of turning a heathen into a believer!

Be Blessed!!!

YOUR FRUIT

Day 80 – The Only One True Gospel

Good Morning my Beautiful Sunshines!

Seed: Our Spiritual Food for Today, comes from: **Galatians 1:6 ESV:** *I am astonished that you are so quickly deserting him who called you in the grace of Christ and are turning to a different gospel—*

Fruit: I'm sure we can all relate to The Apostle Paul's discontent of the church that deserted what they knew to be true, and so quickly turned away from what he taught them. Not only what he taught them, but a privilege to participate in God's truth, and a recipient of His Kingdom.

We were taught the Gospel of Christ Jesus, but some of us will allow any doctrine that fit our lifestyle to replace what we know is the truth!

The enemy will get in our ear, and say anything that he knows we want to hear. If it doesn't teaches us about Jesus; His birth, His works, His crucifixion, and His resurrection, it's not Gospel. And the only way to enter into the kingdom of Heaven is by way of The Christ.

I don't know about you, but after I have left this side, I don't want the cause of me being dismissed from the presence of God, is that I chose to turn from the truth.

Whom will you trust, serve, and believe?

Be Blessed!!!

YOUR FRUIT

Day 81 – Be Like Minded, On One Accord

Good Morning my Beautiful Sunshines!

Seed: Our Spiritual Food for Today, comes from: *1 Corinthians 1:10 ESV: I appeal to you, brothers, by the name of our Lord Jesus Christ, that all of you agree, and that there be no divisions among you, but that you be united in the same mind and the same judgment.*

Fruit: Have you ever wondered why some of the relationships in our household, church, and job; are in chaos?

Scripture says, *And if a house is divided against itself, that house will not be able to stand. (Mark 3:25) KJV*

Although Paul wrote this to the church in Corinth due to some confusion going on in the church; how many experience this same thing in our church, and also in our homes, our relationships, our friends, and on our jobs?

When everyone is not on the same accord, communicating and working out our differences like adults, there will always be division amongst us. Some of us do not want to humble ourselves, and we want to make everything about us. We become self-righteous, and when we have too many self-righteous folks amongst us; the church, our relationships, and the folks we work with, none of it will stand, nor last!

Paul says it best in *Philippians 2:2-3 ESV: complete my joy by being of the same mind, having the same love, being in full accord and of one mind. Do nothing from selfish ambition or conceit, but in humility count others more significant than yourselves.*

When we lower ourselves for the edifying of the Body of Christ, it gives Him so much joy! When our focus is on Christ, and not ourselves we will lift each other up, and not tear down each other! The relationships in our lives will be all the better!

Apply this principle in our church, home, relationships, and our jobs. It will surely fulfill Christ joy, and those that we are in relationships with!

Be Blessed!!!

YOUR FRUIT

Day 82 – We Come To Serve

Good Morning my Beautiful Sunshines!

Seed: Our Spiritual Food for Today, comes from: *Galatians 5:13 ESV: For you were called to freedom, brothers. Only do not use your freedom as an opportunity for the flesh, but through love serve one another.*

Fruit: The Apostle Paul was telling the Galatians to use their freedom, liberty not to be ill willed toward one another, or take the freedom of Christ gift for granted, by indulging in corrupt affections or practices. Which will create distance from The Christ, and have them quarreling with one another, and cause separation in the church, and each other!

What Jesus gave to us; a precious gift, that no other could have given us. Why should we take this gift for granted, by partaking in corruption, misleading people for our own self will, gratification? The gift was given to us to move freely about the earth, to teach the good news of our Father, and what our Lord & Savior, Jesus has done for us! And to edify and glorify Him, and not ourselves.

To really be Christ like, we have to lower ourselves to love and serve one another. Just as Jesus lowered Himself to love and serve us!

Jesus could have just continued to sit at the right hand of our Father, but He was obedient to God's will!

Let's show our appreciation and obedience, and not take our liberties for granted. We may believe that we will not be held accountable if we live, and treat each other that is not pleasing to our Father.

Do not be deceived!

Be Blessed!!!

YOUR FRUIT

Day 83 – Happy To Serve

Good Morning my Beautiful Sunshines!

Seed: Our Spiritual Food for Today, comes from: ***Romans 15:1-3 ESV: We who are strong have an obligation to bear with the failings of the weak, and not to please ourselves. Let each of us please his neighbor for his good, to build him up. For Christ did not please himself, but as it is written, "The reproaches of those who reproached you fell on me."***

Fruit: God is up to something! And when He is up to something, we can be assured it is good!

By us bearing the infirmities of the weak, which can include our friends, neighbors, relatives, children, parents, co-workers, church members, and etc., we are taking on those wonderful Christ like attributes.

Just as Christ lowered Himself to defend His Disciples, and us; when do the same for others, it shows our growth in The Word.

Just as the reproaches or criticism of the Disciples fell on Jesus, when some of John's disciples came to Jesus and asked why were they, and the Pharisees fasting often, but not Jesus Disciples. *(Matthew 9:14 KJV)*. How many know they didn't have to either? If only they realized The Greatness that was in the midst of them, they would have been down with "Team Jesus!"

And we to, must defend and lower the reproaches and criticism of the weak! Even when they come up against us.

I know at times it is not easy to hold our peace, and bite our tongues when someone has wronged us.

But even in one of Jesus darkest moments, He interceded on the behalf of those who crucified Him! Saying, **"Father, forgive them; for they know not what they do." *(Luke 23:34) ESV***

Now if that is not total humility and lowering oneself, I don't know what is!

It was not about Jesus when He descended from His throne!

He said in **Matthew 9:13 ESV:** *'I desire mercy, and not sacrifice.' For I came not to call the righteous, but sinners."*

Again, He answered to the Pharisees because they just couldn't understand why He would sit and eat with publicans and sinners. It is because He never gave anyone the impression that He was above them!

It is in my personal experience that people will be more open and want to learn more from someone they can relate to, and someone who can relate to them.

Putting others before ourselves is truly a Blessing! And it really makes the enemy mad!

Christ like is the way to be!

Be Blessed!!!

YOUR FRUIT

_____

_____

_____

_____

_____

_____

_____

_____

_____

_____

_____

Day 84 – Be Sober To Stand

Good Morning my Beautiful Sunshines!

Seed: Our Spiritual Food for Today, comes from: *1 Peter 1:13 ESV: Therefore, preparing your minds for action, and being sober-minded, set your hope fully on the grace that will be brought to you at the revelation of Jesus Christ.*

Fruit: The Apostle Peter is letting us know that The Word is to make us not only wiser, but also better.

Since we have proclaimed to be Christians, we have a journey that we must fulfill. And when one takes a journey, they take with them everything they need to survive, while on that journey.

We have to gird up, with The Word of God! Be sober, so that we won't get caught off guard and allow ourselves to fall into a trap that the enemy is certainly to set before us. As he certainly does not want us talking and telling others about our Jesus!

And when we run this race for our Lord and Savior, with many war wounds, we have the hope and faith of knowing that our Savior will return to receive those that fought a good fight, for His name sake! Where our wounded bodies, will be replaced with glorified bodies that will last for eternity!

Family gird up, and withstand the wilds of the enemy! Do not slumber, because he will devour you.

Let's run this race for The Son of Man, who died for you, and I!

Be Blessed!!!

YOUR FRUIT

Day 85 – Embrace God's Word, Even If It Hurts

Good Morning my Beautiful Sunshines!

Seed: Our Spiritual Food for Today, comes from: *James 1:19-21 ESV: Know this, my beloved brothers: let every person be quick to hear, slow to speak, slow to anger; for the anger of man does not produce the righteousness of God. Therefore put away all filthiness and rampant wickedness and receive with meekness the implanted word, which is able to save your souls.*

Fruit: Today's spiritual food may prick some hearts, convict some, and it could make you upset! However, let Blessings be added to the readers, hearers, and especially the doers of God's Word!

Some of us don't want to hear God's Word when we don't want to accept, that we need to change our ways. When we know we are not living by God's Word.

We get upset with the messenger, and say they are harsh, judging, and are sinners themselves. And how can they tell us anything about God's Word when they themselves ain't living right! Some of us get out right mad!

But, how do one know they are not living as God would have them to live? It's such a cop out to continue in our sins, to hear and receive the Word of God, when it is only spoken to make us stronger, and all the better.

They are only speaking The Word of God in hopes that we will turn from whatever have us bound in chains. So that we will turn from it, repent, and expose ourselves to God, so that He can take out that which causes us to stumble, and fall short.

Don't get angry at the messenger, receive God's Word with meekness!

Be Blessed!!!

YOUR FRUIT

Day 86 – Love Handed Down Throughout All Generations

Good Morning my Beautiful Sunshines!

Seed: Our Spiritual Food for Today comes from: *Psalm 103:17-18 ESV: But the steadfast love of the L*ORD *is from everlasting to everlasting on those who fear him, and his righteousness to children's children, to those who keep his covenant and remember to do his commandments.*

Fruit: God's mercy and grace is all that matters!

When we recognize who our Father is, fear Him because we know His power, when we get out of order: we will want to walk upright, keep His covenant, and remember to make every effort to live by His commandments.

Generation to generation to generation, and so forth, we have been covered by God's mercy. Pastor mentions on several occasions that we are living off our parent's and grandparent's prayers! But not just their prayers, but the righteous lives they tried to live. We all fall short, so we would be foolish to think our parents and grandparents lived righteously all the time.

But we find ourselves doing the same thing, now that many of us are adults and have children, and grandchildren of our own! We want to try and be the best parent we can be, and raise our children in a way that is pleasing to God.

It is a Blessing to us, and our offspring's to fear God, and live according to His will, and commandments.

Some people believe in generational curses, and I for one do believe in them as well. The only way to break a vicious cycle, is to go about doing things differently.

Some of us know that our parents were off the chain, therefore, what we saw them do, we grow accustom to practicing in the same bad behavior. But in order to change that bad learned behavior, someone has to unlearn that bad behavior, and learn some good behavior. Therefore, breaking that curse.

We want God's steadfast love to go from generation to generation, not His anger, due to our lack of fear, and disobedience.

Be Blessed!!!

YOUR FRUIT

Day 87 – Allow God To Take Control

Good Morning my Beautiful Sunshines!

Seed: Our Spiritual Food for Today, comes from: *Psalm 56:4 ESV: In God, whose word I praise, in God I trust; I shall not be afraid. What can flesh do to me?*

Fruit: God's Word is the truth, it is wisdom, it is knowledge, it is our spiritual food, our convictor, our guide to His Glory, it is righteous, it is just, it's our lifeline! How could we not praise God, and put our trust in Him?

He provided a great guide to living on this side, and what a great reward we will receive by adhering to His Word, when we get to the other side!

When I say God's Word is our lifeline, it is! It teaches us faith, obedience, strength, peace, humility, and many more wonderful attributes!

Often times we are faced with fear of another person, but if we hold on to God's Word of Him being our Protector, and put our trust in Him, those fears cease to exist in us! I've heard many people quote this scripture: **Romans 8:31 ESV: *If God be for us, who can be against us?*** So if we put our trust solely in Him; whatever tries to come up against us will not stand, nor will they win! We all know **Psalm 23:5 ESV**, one verse says, ***You prepare a table before me in the presence of my enemies;***

It might seem like the enemy has won, but we should know that God is working all that out! Yes He is!

Have you ever been in a dangerous situation, and you got out of it alive? You think back and wonder how you got out of that situation? Or when people you thought loved you, turned their backs on you, and you just could not understand why? But then, those very folks that turn their backs on you, have to come to you for help! And they have the look of defeat!

But God! That's how!

Be Blessed!!!

YOUR FRUIT

Day 88 – The Christ Coming To Receive His Bride

Good Morning my Beautiful Sunshines!

Seed: Our Spiritual Food for Today comes from: *1 Thessalonians 4:16-17 ESV: For the Lord himself will descend from heaven with a cry of command, with the voice of an archangel, and with the sound of the trumpet of God. And the dead in Christ will rise first. Then we who are alive, who are left, will be caught up together with them in the clouds to meet the Lord in the air, and so we will always be with the Lord.*

Fruit: Allow me to set some minds at ease!

Now if you can just close your eyes and let the scripture penetrate your heart! Just think about Our Savior Jesus, descending yet again to meet His faithful servants!

Can you see Jesus with His new body, just Glory and those that have long ago left this side, with Him! And they are all just indescribably wonderfully and beautifully made new!

Can you hear that shout that Jesus will send out! Even The dead will recognize His voice!

The dead that faithfully served Him will rise first, because we are 3 dimensional; body, soul, and spirit!

Once we all meet our Wonderful, Amazing, Sweet, Glorious, Precious Lamb in the clouds; He is going to take us Home, to Paradise!!! Forever!!!

Can you see that? I surely can!!!

Bless you Lord for your sacrifice! And giving us the opportunity to live throughout eternity with You!

Where a day is forever!

Be Blessed!!!

YOUR FRUIT

Day 89 – Which Will You Choose

Good Morning my Beautiful Sunshines!

Our Spiritual Food for Today. It comes from me.

Fruit: Whoa! One night at Bible Study had me crying!

We were discussing Christ resurrected body, and when He comes back for us, and our new resurrected bodies! Whether if it is for Heaven eternal, or hell eternal.

What pierced my heart so deeply is when my Pastor said, "Time is going to stop, and either we and/or our love ones will be in heaven or hell forever."

I thought about my family, my children, my friends, and myself! If we don't get it right, and live as Christ, we will be tormented forever! TORMENTED FOREVER! I just can't bear to think about the people I love being tormented forever, why is why I broke down and cried as though I had lost a loved one.

I mean ask yourself. Have you really thought about when Jesus return, and if we are still doing the same thing (sinning), there is nothing but hell eternal for us! And what it will be like?

Please, can you not see that Prophecy is being fulfilled? I love you too much to think about anyone of you being in hell forever!

Let's get this right! Please repent, and accept The Christ as your Lord & Savior before it's too late!

Be Blessed!!!

YOUR FRUIT

Day 90 – No One Before God, Nor After

Good Morning my Beautiful Sunshines!

Seed: Our Spiritual Food for Today comes from: *1 Chronicles 29:11 ESV: Yours, O LORD, is the greatness and the power and the glory and the victory and the majesty, for all that is in the heavens and in the earth is yours. Yours is the kingdom, O LORD, and you are exalted as head above all.*

Fruit: David is acknowledging how great our God is! He is confessing it out loud before many in verse 10.

God is our everything! Whether some of us believe this or not! He created everything, in Heaven and on earth! No one else did!

There are many religions out there that are practiced, and taught! It's not about religion, it's about serving the only One, True, and living God, Yahweh!

All the glory and power, is with Him, and in Him! And no one else!

God will be the only One on this side and the other side that I will give my praises to! It's one of the Great Commandment's! *"You shall have no other gods before me. Exodus 20:3 ESV.*

You don't want to wait to get to the other side and believe, because it will be too late!

We need to exercise our Faith, here and now! It's hard for some to believe with our finite thinking, that a God we can't see, exist! A closed mind, and a closed heart will always keep you in bondage, and imprisoned from getting to know God's greatness!

Scripture says, EVERY knee WILL BOW, and EVERY TONGUE WILL CONFESS, that HE IS LORD! If you wait to do this on the other side, well, let's just say it won't be good for you!

It's time you start praising and worshipping the only true, and living God!

Be Blessed!!!

YOUR FRUIT

ABOUT THE AUTHOR

Bettye Rowe is a Christian that truly loves The Lord, and gave her life to The Christ over thirty years ago. However, it wasn't until four years ago, where she truly sought The Lord, and wanted to have a meaningful and fulfilling relationship with Him. It is her passion to know as much as she can about The Holy Trinity.

She is a divorced mother of four children and six grandchildren, with another grandchild on the way. Currently residing in Rowlett Texas, which is a suburb of Dallas Texas.

This is the first book Bettye has written, but will be publishing a series of "Our Spiritual Food for Today" books. There will be other Christian books that will also be published, and she is currently working on their completion.

Bettye also serves at her church, Zion Baptist Church in Rowlett Texas, where she Co-leads the Singles Ministry - SOLE, the Editor for Zion's monthly newsletter, "ByHisDesign", and serves with other Women of God in the Women Ministry, where they serve hot breakfast to one of the local Battered Women Shelter's.

She will be attending Bible College in the fall of 2013 to further increase her Biblical knowledge. It is her desire to do as God commands His children, and that is to feed His sheep; without watering down, nor taking away from His Truths.

To stay informed of release dates, the latest and greatest of Bettye's other projects, to send her a message on her blog; you may do so on her personal website. The web address is: www.bettyerowe.com

You may also follow her on Facebook @ bettye.rowe (Diva for Christ) and SpiritualFoodForToday
To write: 8301 Lakeview Parkway, Suite 111-153
Rowlett, TX 75088

www.ingramcontent.com/pod-product-compliance
Lightning Source LLC
Chambersburg PA
CBHW022358040426
42450CB00005B/245